AQA GCSE

Leisure & Tourism

Stephen Rickerby

Philip Allan Updates, an imprint of Hodder Education, an Hachette UK company, Market Place, Deddington, Oxfordshire OX15 0SE

Orders
Bookpoint Ltd, 130 Milton Park, Abingdon, Oxfordshire OX14 4SB
tel: 01235 827827
fax: 01235 400401
e-mail: education@bookpoint.co.uk
Lines are open 9.00 a.m.–5.00 p.m., Monday to Saturday, with a 24-hour message answering service. You can also order through the Philip Allan Updates website: www.philipallan.co.uk

© 2010 Stephen Rickerby
ISBN 978-1-84489-649-3

First printed 2010
Impression number   5   4   3   2   1
Year   2014   2013   2012   2011   2010

Printed in Italy

Hachette UK's policy is to use papers that are natural, renewable and recyclable products and made from wood grown in sustainable forests. The logging and manufacturing processes are expected to conform to the environmental regulations of the country of origin.

P01769

Contents

Introduction

Revision suggestions

The most important thing is to be organised! Make sure you know exactly what you will need to learn for the exam. You will be taking either one or two AQA GCSE Leisure and Tourism exams, depending on which AQA qualification you are working towards:

- **Either** GCSE Leisure and Tourism: one exam (Unit 1 Understanding Leisure and Tourism Destinations)
- **Or** GCSE Leisure and Tourism (Double Award): two exams (Unit 1 Understanding Leisure and Tourism Destinations *and* Unit 3 The Business of Leisure and Tourism).

Unit 1 tests what you know and understand about leisure and tourism destinations. You need to know about different types of destination (in the UK and overseas), about what affects people's choice of destination, the visitor attractions offered by destinations and how people travel to them. You only need to revise **one** UK and **one** overseas example of seaside and city destinations. And, you only need to know about **one** overseas ski/snowsports resort and about **one** UK National Park.

Unit 3 is a different style of exam. The paper includes an extract giving information about a leisure and tourism organisation or organisations, and about the business of running them. Some of the questions in the exam will be based on this extract but others will also test how well you can apply the knowledge and understanding of leisure and tourism you have gained from your course. So, it is equally important to revise your Unit 3 work.

Practicing exam-style questions is an excellent way to revise, but make sure you understand the correct answers afterwards.

Using this book

You can use this book for more than just revising for your exams. It also contains valuable sections on controlled assessment. Depending on which qualification (GCSE or GCSE Double Award) you are aiming for, you will complete one or two controlled assessment units (definitely Unit 2 and possibly Unit 4). This book provides you with support for both.

Use each of the topics in Units 1 and 3 to:
- remind yourself what the AQA specification says you have to know and understand
- refresh your memory about the key points of each topic

- bolster your knowledge and understanding of unit content
- gain advice about how to score more marks
- practise exam-style questions

Use each of the topics in the controlled assessment unit sections (Units 2 and 4) to:
- remind you what each unit is about
- build your understanding of controlled assessment in AQA GCSE Leisure and Tourism and how to go about it
- practise controlled assessment-style tasks

Features of this book

Each topic in the book is short and contains the basic knowledge you will need to pass at GCSE. In each topic there are a number of features:

- **What the specification requires**. This gives you an outline of what you need to know and understand to be able to answer exam questions on the topic.

- **In brief**. This is summary of what the topic involves. It states the knowledge requirement in a couple of sentences. For last-minute refreshers, this is what you will need.

- **Revision notes**. This feature gives a more detailed description of the area of knowledge that is absolutely essential for you to know.

- **Speak the language**. This gives the key terms and definitions that you will need for a particular topic. In the exams, there are marks for using the correct technical language. These are highlighted in bold in the text.

- **In a nutshell**. This contains the key points from the topic.

- **Boost your grade**. The more marks you get, the better the grade you will receive. This feature gives handy hints and advice, and suggests other things you might want to mention to gain those extra valuable marks.

- **Test yourself**. This provides a short test on the content of all or part of the topic. It gives you a chance to practise questions that are similar to those you can expect in the exam.

Units 2 and 4 cover controlled assessment, giving advice on the process of controlled assessment and how to prepare for it, as well as suggestions of the kind of controlled assessment tasks you may be asked to do .

At the end of Units 1 and 3, you will find a full practice examination paper, just like the one that you will sit for your GCSE. Suggested answers to the questions are available online at: **www.hodderplus.co.uk/philipallan**

Unit 1
Understanding leisure and tourism destinations

Unit 1 is an examined unit and has a 1-hour written examination. The examination paper consists of both short and longer questions on:

- UK and overseas leisure and tourism destinations
- what makes people decide on destinations
- visitor attractions at destinations and what they offer their customers
- the various ways in which people can travel to destinations
- why sustainability matters and what ecotourism is

Destinations

Leisure and tourism destinations are those places where people go on a business trip, to have fun in their spare time or to visit friends and relatives. Leisure and tourism destinations include:

- beach (or seaside resorts)
- city destinations
- ski and snowsports resorts
- National Parks

These destinations are found in the UK and overseas. You need to know about both UK and overseas beach and city destinations, however you need only revise **one** overseas ski/snowsports resort and **one** UK National Park.

You need to revise so you can:

- outline different types of destination
- describe examples of each type of destination
- describe the difference between long-haul and short-haul destinations

Choice of destination

People choose which destinations they want to visit. Factors that influence their choice of leisure and tourism destinations are:

- the range of products and services on offer
- weather and climate
- personal interests and tastes
- cost
- accessibility
- how destinations are promoted, including promotion by organisations such as transport and accommodation providers, tour operators and travel agents
- events

You need to revise so you can explain the factors that affect people's destination choices

Visitor attractions

Visitor attractions draw tourists to leisure and tourism destinations. There are many types of visitor attraction. A natural feature, for example a waterfall such as Niagara Falls, is a visitor attraction. So are historic monuments such as Stonehenge and the Great Pyramid at Giza in Egypt. Equally, theme parks such as Alton Towers and Disneyland Paris are visitor attractions, as are museums, art galleries, and major sports and entertainment venues such as London's O2 Arena.

You need to know about different types of visitor attraction, including examples of each type, in the UK and overseas. You need to understand how different attractions try to attract customers and how they meet customers' needs during the visit.

You need to revise so you can:

- describe the range of leisure activities available at UK and overseas visitor attractions
- describe and explain why visitor attractions try to meet the needs of different customer types
- explain in the exam how a visitor attraction you have not studied in your course seeks to attract different customer types

The Great Pyramid at Giza in Egypt

Travelling to destinations

People need to travel to reach leisure and tourism destinations and attractions. The trips they make range from short local journeys, perhaps to visit the local leisure centre, to international journeys to and from overseas destinations, for example for a holiday in a beach or seaside resort abroad.

You need to know about:

- available methods of travel to leisure and tourism destinations and why people choose them
- different ways in which domestic and international tourists move around, enter and leave the UK, including modes, routes, terminals and gateways
- advantages and disadvantages of different ways of travelling for different types of customers and journeys

You need to revise so you can:

- explain the advantages and disadvantages of different ways of travelling for different types of customer
- explain why some travel options may appeal to some customers more than to others
- evaluate how well they do so
- describe the range of different travel options to UK and overseas destinations from your home area

Sustainability and ecotourism

Sustainability is very important in leisure and tourism. Visiting destinations sustainably means doing so now in ways that do not harm their future, the future environment or the future of the people who live in leisure and tourism destinations.

Ecotourism is visiting destinations because of their natural appeal while doing minimal harm to the environment and the lives of people who live there.

The impacts of tourism on destinations can be positive and negative. Sustainable tourism (including ecotourism) aims to maximise positive impacts while minimising negative ones. Tourism impacts are:

- economic
- social
- environmental

You need to revise so you can:

- describe and explain the positive and negative impacts of tourism and different views about those
- evaluate tourism's impacts on the environment
- explain what sustainability is and why it is important in leisure and tourism in the UK and internationally
- explain the meaning and aims of ecotourism and responsible tourism
- evaluate how well responsible tourism recognises similarities and differences of attitudes and cultures between visitors and local communities

Topic 1
Beach (or seaside) resorts

What the specification requires

You need to be able to describe examples of beach (or seaside) resorts found in the UK and overseas.

In brief

UK seaside resorts developed largely in the nineteenth century when the development of railways allowed **domestic tourists** living in industrial towns to visit them. For example, tourists from Leeds and York could travel by train to Scarborough. Since the mid-twentieth century, fewer people have spent their annual holidays in UK seaside towns because they have been able to afford to travel to sunnier beach resorts abroad.

Many overseas beach (or seaside) resorts visited by **out-bound tourists** from the UK are located around the Mediterranean Sea and in the following areas:
- northern and western France (for example, Normandy, Brittany and the Vendée)
- the Algarve in Portugal
- the Canary Islands
- Asia (Goa and Thailand are destinations popular with UK visitors)
- the United States, especially Florida
- the Caribbean

Mass tourism happens when many tourists travel to a destination at once. The availability of **package holidays** in the 1960s encouraged mass tourism from the UK to Mediterranean destinations such as seaside resorts in Spain.

Revision notes

UK

Scarborough is an example of a UK beach resort:
- It is a seaside resort with two beaches and is located on the North Yorkshire coast at the end of the railway line from the historic city destination of York. York is about 50 kilometres southwest of Scarborough.
- South Bay is the more developed, busier part of the resort of Scarborough. As well as a sandy beach, there is a harbour and an historic **spa**. Originally the spa was a place where tourists

came to drink natural mineral water for their health. Nowadays it is used to host concerts and conferences.

- Pleasure cruises operate out of the harbour. Tourists can enjoy trips along the coast on boats such as the *Coronia* and the *Regal Lady*. The foreshore is the sea-front area that stretches from the harbour south to the spa. Here tourists will find amusement arcades, fish-and-chip restaurants, ice-cream parlours and some pubs. It is the busiest part of the resort.
- On the headland that separates Scarborough's two bays there is a ruined castle which is a visitor attraction. To the north is North Bay, which offers quieter attractions than South Bay, including another sandy beach. There are two parks here: Peasholm Park, which includes a boating lake, and Northstead Manor Gardens with a miniature railway. Tourists can ride the miniature railway to Scalby at the far end of the bay.
- Scarborough's Stephen Joseph Theatre is famous nationally for its theatre-in-the-round auditorium.
- Accommodation in Scarborough comprises a mixture of larger hotels and smaller guest houses, some of which have been converted into self-catering apartments. Hotels include the Grand and the St Nicholas. Such establishments cater for coach parties and business people as well as leisure tourists. Columbus Ravine, near Peasholm Park, is one street in particular that has many guest houses.

Speak the language

domestic tourist — someone who visits a destination that is in her/his own country

out-bound tourist — someone who travels out of a country to visit a destination in another country

mass tourism — organised travel to a destination by large numbers of visitors

package holiday — a holiday that is sold as one product for a single price, although it is usually made up of several elements

spa — a leisure facility that people visit for health or beauty reasons. In the past, and still sometimes today, people went to spas to 'take the waters'. Modern spas offer a range of health and beauty treatments

tourist-receiving areas — regions that attract large numbers of visitors who live elsewhere

The Grand Hotel in Scarborough overlooking the foreshore

Overseas

Examples of beach (seaside) resorts found in **tourist-receiving areas** overseas are listed in the table. Note that beach (or seaside) resorts are towns. So, for example, Negril is a resort whereas Jamaica is a tourist-receiving area.

Many tourists from the UK buy package holidays to overseas beach (or seaside) destinations.

Tourist-receiving area	Example of beach (or seaside) resort
Mediterranean	Chania, Crete
Northern and western France	La Baule, southern Brittany
The Algarve	Praia da Luz
Canary Islands	Playa das Americas
Thailand	Phuket
Florida	St Petersburg
Caribbean	Negril, Jamaica

In a nutshell

Scarborough is one example of a UK beach (or seaside) resort. Like many such resorts, it grew rapidly in the nineteenth century as people were able to travel to it by rail. Since the middle of the twentieth century, the resort has declined as a holiday destination, although it is still popular for short breaks and day trips. Its attractions are typical for a beach (or seaside) resort in the UK.

Overseas beach (or seaside) resorts popular with UK tourists are found in different parts of the world including the Mediterranean and the Far East. Since the mid-twentieth century, out-bound tourism from the UK to overseas destinations, including beach destinations, has grown. Travel to destinations beyond Europe (including in the USA, Thailand and the Caribbean) became more common from the late-twentieth century onwards.

Test yourself

1 (a) Where is Scarborough?

  (b) Why do tourists go there?

  (c) How can people get to Scarborough?

2 What is 'mass tourism' and when did it start?

3 What is meant by 'domestic tourists' and 'out-bound tourists'?

Boost your grade

When you are asked to describe a destination such as a beach (or seaside) resort, make sure you include information that is specifically about that place. Include the names of places and facilities. Write a 'somewhere' answer not a 'nowhere' answer.

There is likely to be a variety of ways in which UK tourists can reach an overseas beach (or seaside) destination. You should stick to real routes and methods of travel that tourists actually use.

City destinations

What the specification requires

You need to be able to describe examples of city destinations in the UK and overseas.

In brief

Many cities in the UK promote themselves as historic destinations. For example, Durham, Exeter and York are cathedral cities. Bath is famous for its Roman Baths and the Georgian architecture of its streets, such as the Royal Crescent.

In recent years many industrial cities have promoted their more modern historical and cultural attractions. For example, Halifax has marketed its Piece Hall art gallery, where the Eureka interactive museum for children adds to the town's tourist appeal. Newcastle upon Tyne has acquired an image as a 'party city'. It attracts tourists who want to enjoy its nightlife, as well as more cultural attractions such as the Baltic art gallery and Sage music venue in neighbouring Gateshead. Edinburgh, the historic capital of Scotland, has the additional appeal of its annual arts festival.

Overseas city destinations that are particularly popular among out-bound tourists from the UK include New York, Paris, Amsterdam, Rome and Barcelona. However, most major cities in the world attract some tourism from the UK for leisure, for business purposes or for visits to friends and relatives.

In recent years, short break holidays to city destinations have grown in popularity, particularly to European cities such as Prague and Madrid, but also further afield across the Atlantic Ocean, especially to New York.

Revision notes

UK

As the UK's capital city, London has a broad appeal and is the country's major destination for **in-bound tourism**. Leisure visitors, including many domestic tourists, are drawn to London because of:
- historic attractions, such as the Tower of London
- royal connections, such as Buckingham Palace

- famous sights, such as Tower Bridge
- cultural attractions, such as the British Museum and Tate gallery
- nightlife and shopping, such as in the West End

London is also a major destination for purposes of tourism other than leisure, notably business tourism. The city's hotels and conference centres host many business meetings daily and its major exhibitions and trade fairs attract business tourists from around the world. The 2012 Olympics will be a major tourist as well as sporting event.

Overseas

New York City is a major overseas city destination for tourists from the UK. The city's location in the northeast of the USA makes it closer to the UK than some other American cities such as Chicago and Los Angeles, although Boston is actually closer still.

New York — the city that never sleeps

Gary/Fotolia

The appeal of New York for UK tourists lies in the excitement of a city that seems constantly on the move. It has been called 'the city that never sleeps'. Attractions that are popular with tourists to New York include:
- the Statue of Liberty
- skyscrapers, including the Empire State Building and Rockefeller Centre
- Central Park
- Brooklyn Bridge
- Times Square
- art galleries, such as MOMA (Metropolitan Museum of Modern Art) and the Guggenheim
- theatres and nightlife on and around Broadway
- iconic stores, such as Bloomingdales, Macy's and Tiffany's

New York City has five boroughs, although most tourism activities are concentrated on the central island borough of Manhattan. New York is a melting pot of ethnicities and cultures from all over the world. The cultural life, heritage and food of ethnic neighbourhoods such as Chinatown, Little Italy and Harlem are part of the city's appeal for many tourists.

Speak the language

in-bound tourism — visiting a destination in one country having travelled from another country

positive economic impacts — the financial and employment benefits that tourism brings

transport modes — different forms of transport

In a nutshell

UK city destinations include, but are not confined to, the country's many historical cities. Examples of city destinations include York, Halifax and, the biggest, London. City councils are keen to promote towns as leisure and tourism destinations because of the **positive economic impacts** that visitors bring.

City destinations visited by UK tourists overseas are found all over the world.

Today there are more budget airline flights and a greater availability of short break holidays than ever before. These changes are closely related to the expanding range of overseas city destinations visited by UK tourists, especially in Europe and nearby regions of North Africa such as Morocco. New York City is one example of a major overseas destination for UK tourists that is located outside Europe.

Boost your grade

Remember:
- Many tourists travel to overseas city destinations (especially those outside Western Europe) by air. Bear in mind, though, that there are various ways of doing this — different airlines, different routes and different dates and times, for example.
- For city destinations in Western Europe, ferry, car and train are alternative **transport modes**.
- Research a city destination that means something to you — perhaps one that is local or that you have visited as a tourist.

Test yourself

1 For one UK city destination, state what attracts tourists to visit it.

2 Give two different ways in which in-bound tourists can travel to one UK city destination.

3 How are the growth of budget airlines and UK tourist visits to overseas city destinations linked?

4 Why are holidays to city destinations often short breaks?

What the specification requires

You need to know about an overseas ski/snowsports resort.

In brief

A holiday to a ski and snowsports resort is an example of a **specialist holiday**. Ski and snowsports resorts abroad that are popular with UK tourists are mainly in Europe and North America, although there are some further afield, for example in Australia and New Zealand.

The Alps is a European mountain range that crosses the borders of France, Italy, Switzerland and Austria. In the Alps there are many ski/snowsports resorts.

The Valle d'Aosta is an Alpine Valley in northwestern Italy (see map), just across the border from France. In the eastern part of the valley there are a number of ski resorts, including Cervinia.

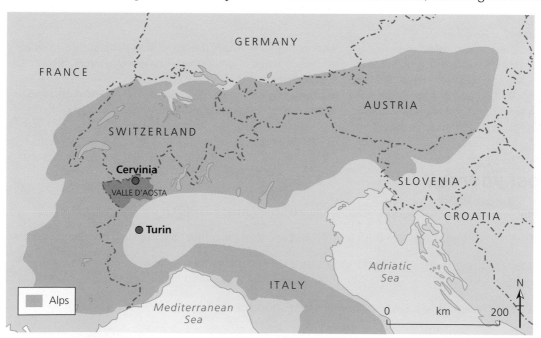

Location of the Alps and the Valle d'Aosta

Revision notes

Cervinia is one of the highest resorts in the Alps, at an altitude of over 2,000 m above sea level. It is two hours drive from the Italian **gateway** city of Turin with its **international airport**.

As well as skiing, tourists also take part in other snowsports such as snowboarding. Both cross-country and downhill skiing are available and there are motorised skidoos for hire.

Facilities provided for skiers and snowboarders at Cervinia include 60 downhill runs or **pistes**, 31 ski-lifts and five cable cars which connect to other nearby resorts, and a snowboard park.

Après-ski activities are an important part of skiing and snowsports holidays. In Cervinia there are numerous restaurants, cafés, bars and night-clubs to cater for demand. Other leisure facilities include a bowling alley, a natural ice rink for skating, a swimming pool and a cinema. The jobs provided by these facilities are a positive economic impact of tourism for ski resorts, at least during the season.

The **seasonality** of **tourism flow** is an issue for ski resorts. It is more difficult to encourage tourism in the summer when much of the snow melts. Tourists do still visit to admire the scenery and take part in leisure activities such as hiking, but there are fewer of them.

Speak the language

specialist holiday — a holiday centred around one leisure activity, such as skiing or golfing

gateway — a point of entry into a country for in-bound tourists

international airport — an airport from which airlines operate flights to and from other countries

piste — a snow slope in a ski resort that has been prepared for skiing and/or snowboarding

après-ski — evening leisure activities provided in ski and snowsports resorts

seasonality — variations from one time of year to another, for example between summer and winter

tourism flow — the volume of tourists visiting a destination. This often varies according to season

Da tus/Foto ia

Ski resorts provide specialist facilities for skiing and snowboarding

Ski/snowsports resorts are located in mountainous areas. The Alps are a major region for ski resorts in Europe. Ski resorts provide specialist leisure facilities for skiing and snowsports, including pistes and ski-lifts. Leisure and tourism organisations in ski resorts also offer a variety of après-ski facilities. Ski tourism brings economic benefits to ski resorts but the seasonality of tourism flow can be an issue.

Test yourself

1 Outline the range of leisure facilities provided by a ski resort such as Cervinia.

2 Give two different ways by which tourists from the UK can travel to Cervinia.

3 Where is Cervinia?

4 What is it about Cervinia that attracts UK tourists?

Boost your grade   The Ski Club of Great Britain is a valuable source of information about skiing as a leisure and tourism activity. See **www.skiclub.co.uk**

A UK National Park

What the specification requires

You need to be able to describe a UK National Park.

In brief

National Parks are large areas of attractive countryside that are legally protected for the enjoyment of the public. Many leisure activities, often with an outdoor aspect, are provided by leisure and tourism organisations in the UK's National Parks. For example:

- walking
- angling
- sailing
- canoeing
- climbing
- cycling
- horse riding and pony trekking
- painting and photography
- bird watching

Because of the natural beauty of their landscapes, their wildlife and the wide range of leisure activities they offer, National Parks are major tourist destinations in the UK. The map shows the locations of the UK's National Parks.

National Parks in England and Wales

Revision notes

Each National Park is the responsibility of its own **National Park Authority**. The first parks to be designated by the government were the Peak District, Lake District, Snowdonia and Dartmoor.

The most recent designation was given to the New Forest National Park in 2005. In 2008 there were 14 National Parks in the UK, with the South Downs under consideration as a possible fifteenth.

The Pembrokeshire Coast National Park (PCNP) is in southwest Wales. It is unique among the UK's National Parks because it is entirely coastal. The Pembrokeshire Coast Path, which passes through the National Park, is one of the UK's 15 **National Trails** (the Pennine Way is another) and is a major tourist attraction. Coastal scenery in the Pembrokeshire Coast National Park includes rugged cliffs, sandy beaches and attractive, wooded river estuaries.

Historic attractions in the PCNP include Castell Henllys Iron Age Fort, between the towns of Fishguard and Cardigan, and the Medieval Carew Castle, which is further south, between Tenby and Pembroke.

In a nutshell

The UK has 14 National Parks. They are large areas of countryside conserved for the public's enjoyment. The Pembrokeshire Coast National Park is one of the UK's National Parks. It has scenic and historic attractions and is located on the southwest Wales coast.

tbc/Fotolia

The Pembrokeshire Coast National Park is entirely coastal

Test yourself

1 What is a National Park?

2 What is it about the Pembrokeshire Coast National Park that attracts tourists?

3 Give travel instructions to the Pembrokeshire Coast National Park for a tourist wishing to arrive there from your home area.

Boost your grade

Do not confuse National Park with **Area of Outstanding Natural Beauty** (AONB), which is a separate, different countryside conservation designation. While they are similarly protected, AONBs do not have a designated authority in charge of each one. Instead, they are looked after by local councils and communities working together as partners.

Topic 5
Destination choices: products and services

What the specification requires

You need to understand how products and services affect people's destination choices.

In brief

The range of leisure and tourism products and services on offer is one factor that people consider when they are deciding which destination to visit. This includes travel products and services that they may choose to use to reach a destination. Their choice of destination is likely to be influenced by how easy (and cheap) it will be to travel there as well as by what there is on offer in the destination.

Revision notes

Questions people consider are:
- What accommodation is available in the destination?
- What attractions and activities are there?
- What are the travel options?

All-inclusive hotels are most frequently found in long-haul beach (or seaside) resorts. The customer pays a single bill, normally in advance. This one-off charge covers accommodation, meals, drinks and leisure activities at the hotel. Sometimes, however, more expensive optional activities, such as diving, gourmet restaurant meals and branded drinks, do attract an additional charge.

Many all-inclusive hotel guests have bought a package holiday, including the hotel, airline flight and airport transfer.

Travel agents advertise special deals to attract customers

The principal advantage of an all-inclusive arrangement is that the entire holiday is paid for. Guests can relax without having to think about money at all.

An example of an all-inclusive holiday is a two-week package holiday to Beaches Hotel in Negril, Jamaica. The price that customers pay for this holiday includes not only their flight, accommodation and transfers (an ordinary package holiday would do that) but also meals, drinks and activities such as water sports.

However, all-inclusive hotels are a leisure and tourism **issue**. There are advantages and disadvantages for both the environment and local people in a destination. All-inclusive holidays have attracted some controversy as a result.

The range of products and services on offer is one factor that affects people's destination choices. There are others, and together they are all part of the eventual decision. For example, cost, personal interests and personal tastes are other factors. They affect how people view the range of products and services on offer when they choose a destination to visit.

In a nutshell

The range of products and services on offer is one factor that can affect people's choice of leisure and tourism destination. Products and services offered include accommodation, attractions and activities at destinations, as well as the travel options customers can use to reach them.

Test yourself

1 What are leisure and tourism products and services?

2 Identify two sets of products and services that can affect people's choice of leisure and tourism destination.

3 How does the range of products and services on offer affect people's destination choice?

4 Give two other factors that can affect how people view the range of products and services on offer when they pick a destination to visit.

Boost your grade Don't worry about what is a product and what is a service. You are not expected to be able to differentiate between them.

Topic 6
Destination choices: weather and climate

What the specification requires

You need to be able to explain how weather and climate affect people's destination choices.

In brief

Weather and **climate** can affect people's choice of destination. Outdoor leisure activities and holidays are particularly affected, especially when the latter are to beach (or seaside) or to ski/snowsports resorts. Activities such as windsurfing and skiing are dependent on wind and snowfall. However, most customers prefer fine weather when they visit a destination of any type.

Revision notes

Beach (or seaside) resort holidays overseas are sometimes referred to as **sun, sea and sand** holidays. During the 1960s in the UK there was a boom in package holidays to Mediterranean destinations, when many British tourists visited beach (or seaside) resorts in countries such as Spain and Greece for the first time. Weather and climate were an important factor then and remain so today. Millions of holiday-makers from the UK continue to travel to Mediterranean destinations such as Praia da Luz (Portuguese Algarve), Benidorm (Costa Blanca, Spain) and Ayia Napa (Cyprus) in search of summer sunshine.

Mediterranean resorts offer reliably hot and sunny weather

The climate of the Mediterranean is characterised by hot, dry summers and mild, wet winters. A typical day in a destination with a Mediterranean climate has hot, sunny weather, and it was the hotter, sunnier climate of the Mediterranean in summer that first appealed to people from the UK. As resorts in the Mediterranean developed, the mildness (if not the dampness) of the winters also proved attractive to **out-of-season** visitors.

Mass domestic tourism in the UK began in the nineteenth century with railway trips to the seaside. By the mid-twentieth century large numbers of British people were taking annual seaside holidays in UK beach (or seaside) resorts such as Blackpool, Scarborough and Brighton. However, weather and climate were an issue. Although the British climate is equable (lacks extremes), summers are not very warm compared with the Mediterranean and the weather is notoriously variable. A family taking a week's or fortnight's holiday to a UK seaside resort could not rely on fine, warm, sunny weather and many beach holidays were spoiled by rain and wind. Therefore, Mediterranean alternatives were very attractive when they became readily available from the 1960s onwards.

In a nutshell

Weather and climate affect people's choice of destination. Reliably hot and sunny weather is a major deciding factor for British leisure tourists to travel to overseas beach (or seaside) resorts in the Mediterranean. Other factors, however, influence which destination within the Mediterranean they choose.

Test yourself

1 Explain how two leisure activities are dependent on the weather.

2 Why did mass tourism lead to the Mediterranean tourism boom in the 1960s?

Boost your grade People have different views about weather and climate. Some enjoy hot, sunny weather but others find it uncomfortable. Sight-seeing in a city destination can be tiring for a UK tourist in the heat of a Mediterranean summer or a tropical day.

Topic 7
Destination choices: personal interests and tastes

What the specification requires

You need to understand how personal interests and tastes influence people's choice of destination.

In brief

The range of products and services offered by a destination will appeal to a particular customer only if they match her/his interests or personal tastes. People don't visit destinations they don't find appealing.

People's particular interests affect their choice of where to visit. Leisure and tourism organisations provide special interest day-trips and holidays. Special interest holidays centre on a leisure activity that customers particularly enjoy and want to spend a large part of their holiday pursuing.

Sailing is an activity many people enjoy pursuing on holiday

João Freitas/Fotolia

Revision notes

Examples of special interest holidays include:

- skiing and snowsports
- climbing, trekking or walking
- angling
- sailing and other water sports holidays
- diving
- golfing
- painting, cookery and wine tours
- bird-watching

Special interest day-trips are organised to allow customers to attend **events**. For example, coach or train operators often organise excursions to sporting occasions such as race meetings.

Special interest holidays are provided by specialist companies as well as by larger general tour operators such as Thomson, First Choice and Kuoni. Golfing holidays to Portugal, for instance, are offered by specialist operators including Algarve Golf (UK) and Golfbreaks.com.

In a nutshell

Personal interests and tastes can affect destination choices. The internet has made it easier for people to search for holidays that match their personal tastes and interests.

People's particular leisure interests and an opportunity to attend an organised event are factors that can affect destination choices. Someone with a special interest such as playing golf or sailing may visit a destination because of the opportunity to pursue their interest there.

Test yourself

1 How can personal interests and tastes affect people's choice of leisure and tourism destination?

2 Give two examples of special interest holidays.

Boost your grade

Personal interests and tastes are two of a range of factors that can affect people's choice of destination. This means that the cheapest options will not always be those that are chosen.

An event will attract visitors to a destination because of their special interest, but event organisers must provide for the needs of general visitors too.

Topic 8
Destination choices: costs and accessibility

What the specification requires

You need to know how people's destination choices can be affected by costs and by accessibility.

In brief

The cost of a trip is a major factor in a decision about which destination to visit. While the range of products and services on offer may appeal to a customer, they will only choose to visit a destination if the cost of doing so is considered sufficiently low.

The accessibility of a destination can also can affect people's decisions about which to visit.

Revision notes

The introduction of budget airlines has had an impact on the costs of visiting many short-haul city destinations. Budget airline flights have made it possible to travel to and from the UK more cheaply than previously.

British Airways is a **flag carrier airline**. Ryanair and easyJet are examples of budget airlines. Budget airlines offer cheaper fares because of their **no-frills** policies.

The cost of flights from the UK to overseas destinations varies with:
- departure airport
- date and day of the week
- time of day
- demand from customers
- events at the destination, for example trade fairs and major sports events
- special promotions

Budget airlines have brought down the cost of travelling

The flight from the UK to a destination airport is not the only travel cost incurred by tourists.

Accessibility is the ease of reaching a destination. Factors affecting accessibility include:

- location
- transport links
- measures taken to meet the special needs of visitors

Visitors are unlikely to decide to visit a destination just because it is accessible. They need a reason for wanting to go there in the first place — an attractive range of leisure and tourism products and services, for example. Promotion is another important factor in bringing to their attention the range of leisure and tourism products and services on offer.

In a nutshell

Cost is one factor that can affect people's destination choices. Budget airlines have brought down the cost of travelling to city destinations abroad. The internet has made it easier for people to compare costs of various ways of travelling to different destinations.

Test yourself

1 Why does the cost of flights from the UK to overseas destinations vary?

2 How does cost affect people's choice of leisure and tourism destination?

3 Why is accessibility for visitors a factor in destination choice?

4 Give two ways in which destinations can improve accessibility.

Boost your grade

Cost is only one factor that can affect people's choice of destination. The cheapest options will not always be chosen. The cheapest flights may be at inconvenient times, for example.

Accessibility can also affect people's choice of overseas, as well as of UK, destinations.

Accessibility is how easy it is for visitors to reach a destination.

Topic 9
Destination choices: promotion and events

What the specification requires

You need to be able to explain how promotion and events can affect people's choice of destination.

In brief

How destinations are promoted can affect people's decisions about which to visit. **Events** can also affect people's choice of where to visit. Leisure and tourism organisations provide special interest day-trips and holidays. Special interest holidays centre on a leisure activity that customers particularly enjoy and want to spend a large part of their holiday pursuing.

Revision notes

Promotion is bringing leisure and tourism products and services to the attention of potential customers.

Leisure and tourism organisations, including **regional tourist boards**, promote destinations using materials that include advertisements, **flyers**, brochures and websites. The Northumbria Tourist Board, for example, is the regional tourist board for the northeast of England, including the historic city destination of Durham.

There are eight regional tourist boards in England:
- South West Tourism
- Tourism South East
- Visit London
- East of England Tourist Board

Speak the language

event — a single, specially organised occasion that acts as a temporary visitor attraction. Sports matches and competitions, concerts, festivals and fêtes are examples

regional tourist board — a government-funded authority responsible for the development of tourism in a particular area

flyer — a piece of promotional material that consists of a single, unfolded sheet of paper

Part of the Visit Cambridge website

- The Heart of England Tourist Board
- Northumbria Tourist Board
- Yorkshire Tourist Board
- North West of England Tourist Board

Northern Ireland has its own tourist board. Visit Wales and Visit Scotland undertake similar roles, promoting tourism to destinations in Wales and Scotland.

Special interest day-trips are often organised for customers to attend events. Coach or train operators, for example, often organise excursions to sporting occasions such as race meetings, or to events such as Clothes Show Live at the National Exhibition Centre (NEC) in Birmingham.

In a nutshell

Promotion is an important factor that can affect people's destination choices. Promotion is how the appeal of a destination is brought to people's attention. In the UK, tourist boards are concerned with the promotion and development of tourism to particular regions.

Events can also affect destination choices. Events such as Clothes Show Live or sporting occasions attract visitors to the destinations where they are held.

Test yourself

1 How can promotion affect people's destination choice?

2 (a) What is meant by an 'event'?

　　(b) Give three examples of events.

3 Explain why people's choice of destination can be influenced by events.

Boost your grade An event will attract visitors to a destination because of their special interest, but event organisers must provide for the needs of general visitors too.

Topic 10
Natural attractions

What the specification requires

You need to know about natural attractions and the leisure activities they offer.

In brief

Natural attractions appeal to visitors because of their physical beauty. Waterfalls, mountains, valleys and canyons, volcanoes and unusual rock formations, such as the Giant's Causeway in Northern Ireland, are examples of this type of visitor attraction.

Revision notes

Natural attractions can be any feature of the physical landscape. As well as waterfalls and caverns they include:
- mountains and volcanoes
- lakes
- glaciers
- unusual rock formations
- coral reefs

Leisure activities available at natural attractions vary but typically include sightseeing, active physical activities such as walking, climbing and cycling, and more passive activities such as bird-watching and angling. Some activities, such as the woodland walk to the falls at High Force (County Durham), are offered to visitors by leisure and tourism organisations, others are enjoyed free of charge by individuals acting independently, for example walking the Pennine Way. Public footpaths do, however, have to be maintained (typically by the local council) to allow this type of leisure activity.

Giant's Causeway in Northern Ireland

Natural attractions stimulate sightseeing tourism to countryside areas. Leisure and tourism organisations provide facilities where customers spend money. This benefits the local economy.

Different leisure and tourism organisations are owned and funded in different ways. They are run with different aims. Leisure and tourism organisations can be owned privately by companies or individuals, by the public (often through local councils or regional tourist boards) or by registered charities. This means that any one leisure and tourism organisation belongs to one of three sectors of the economy:

1 **Private sector**: **commercial** organisations that are owned by individual people or by shareholders. Their funding comes from sales and admissions and they operate to make a profit. Most travel and tourism organisations and many leisure organisations belong to this sector. Examples include travel agents, hotels and many visitor attractions.

2 **Public sector**: organisations that are owned by the state on behalf of the public. They are at least partly funded from taxes and they are run to provide services for the public benefit. Examples include tourist information centres and leisure centres.

3 **Voluntary sector**: charitably owned organisations that are funded in part by donations. They operate to further the good cause for which the charity was set up. Examples include youth hostels and some visitor attractions such as those run by the National Trust.

In a nutshell

Natural attractions appeal to visitors because of their physical beauty. Examples include waterfalls such as High Force, and rock formations including the Giant's Causeway in the UK and the Grottes de Thouzon caverns in France.

Test yourself

1 What is the meaning of:

(a) a commercial leisure attraction?

(b) a voluntary leisure and tourism organisation?

2 Give three examples of the activities available at natural attractions.

Boost your grade You need to know about one natural attraction in the UK and one overseas natural attraction. Understand what it is about each that appeals to visitors and what leisure activities are available.

What the specification requires

You need to understand what historic sites are and what they offer to visitors.

In brief

Historic sites are places such as ancient monuments and old buildings that have become attractions for visitors.

Examples of different types of historic sites are:
- stately homes and palaces
- historically significant places of worship, such as cathedrals, mosques and temples
- abbeys, priories and monasteries
- castles and other fortifications
- other ancient sites, such as prehistoric stone circles and cities that date from previous civilisations

Revision notes

Historic sites are old buildings and monuments that have become visitor attractions. They were not built to be attractions.

Examples of different types of historic attraction in the UK and overseas are given in the table overleaf.

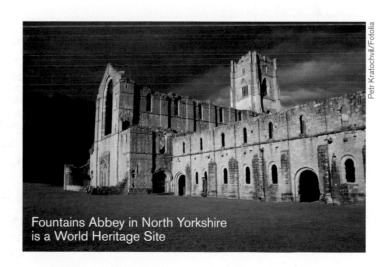

Fountains Abbey in North Yorkshire is a World Heritage Site

Petr Kratochvil/Fotolia

Type of historic attraction	UK examples	Overseas examples
Stately homes and palaces	Beaulieu Buckingham Palace	Sanssouci, Berlin Palace of Versailles, France
Historic cathedrals, mosques, temples, etc.	Canterbury Cathedral York Minster	Dome of the Rock, Jerusalem The Golden Temple, Amritsar
Abbeys, priories and monasteries	Fountains Abbey	Meteora monasteries, Greece
Castles and other fortifications	Hadrian's Wall Edinburgh Castle	The Great Wall of China
Other ancient sites	Stonehenge	Machu Picchu, Peru

Built attractions are usually modern sites that were specifically constructed to attract visitors. **Heritage attractions** include built attractions such as museums. For example, Beamish Museum in the UK is a heritage attraction.

In a nutshell

Historic sites are one type of visitor attraction. They can be found in the UK and overseas. They include old buildings used for worship, castles and palaces, as well as other ancient sites such as prehistoric stone circles like Stonehenge.

Leisure activities available at historic sites include sightseeing, but others such as taking part in historical re-enactments are also offered by the leisure and tourism organisations that operate them.

Test yourself

1 (a) Identify five different types of historic site attraction.

(b) Give one UK and one overseas example of each type.

2 Describe the range of leisure activities available at one UK historic site attraction.

Boost your grade

World Heritage Sites are places that are so important to the world's heritage and culture that they are specially listed for conservation by the United Nations. In North Yorkshire, Fountains Abbey is a UK historic site attraction that, like Durham Cathedral (and Castle) in Durham city, is also a World Heritage Site.

Topic 12
Theme parks

What the specification requires

You need to be able to describe theme parks in the UK and overseas.

In brief

Theme parks are visitor attractions that include rides. They occupy large sites. Some theme parks have a clear theme that pervades the attraction. Examples include Walt Disney World and Disneyland theme parks in Florida, California, Paris, Tokyo and Hong Kong where rides, buildings and characters are based around the theme of Walt Disney films. Legoland Windsor in the UK, the original Legoland in Denmark and the more recently developed Legoland California and Legoland Deutschland (Germany) are all centred around the theme of Lego construction toys.

Revision notes

Some theme parks do not have a clear theme. The UK's Alton Towers, for example, is a theme park without a theme. It is a theme park because it is a large visitor attraction whose appeal is based on rides. Its operators haven't found it necessary to have a central unifying theme in the way that Disneyland Paris, Legoland Windsor or Camelot in northwest England have.

Alton Towers

Poster for Alton Towers' 'Oblivion' ride

Theme parks are one type of **built attraction**. These are visitor attractions that were specifically built to attract visitors. As well as theme parks, there are many other examples of built attractions, including the London Eye and the Spinnaker Tower in Portsmouth. Public museums and art galleries are also types of built attraction. Part of their purpose is to conserve old objects, documents and works of art but they have also been developed to display these to visitors.

Speak the language

theme park — a large visitor attraction whose appeal to visitors is primarily based on mechanical rides

built attraction — an attraction that was purpose-built to be a visitor attraction

Spinnaker Tower in Portsmouth

Giuliano Maciocci/Fotolia

In a nutshell

Theme parks and built attractions are two types of visitor attraction. Both offer a range of leisure activities to visitors.

Test yourself

1 What is meant by

   (a) a 'theme park'?

   (b) a 'built attraction'?

2 Name three examples of theme parks.

Boost your grade Make sure you also learn about types of built attractions other than theme parks — places such as museums and galleries for example.

Topic 13
Sports and entertainment venues

What the specification requires

You need to know about sports and entertainment venues.

In brief

Major sports and entertainment **venues** attract visitors primarily to watch sports events and to attend shows. Such venues include:

- **stadia**
- racecourses
- **arenas**
- theatres, concert halls and opera houses

Revision notes

Many major venues are so famous that visitors are attracted to them even when sports and entertainment events are not in progress. They are sightseeing attractions in themselves. Such venues often operate tours as result, frequently using **audioguides**. Tours are an important way for venues to generate extra income. A football stadium, for example, may host a major match only once every week or two — and then only (or mostly) during the football season. The rest of the time the ground would stand empty and there would be no income to maintain the facility or to help it be profitable. **Secondary purposes** are therefore vital to keep such facilities running.

Speak the language

venue — a leisure facility such as a stadium or arena where events are held or shows are staged

stadia — the plural of stadium, a large outdoor facility where sports events such as football matches are held

arena — a large indoor venue

audioguide — an electronic device that replays a recorded commentary through headphones for visitors touring an attraction

secondary purpose — a use of a leisure facility other than its main function, for example staging a rock concert at a football ground

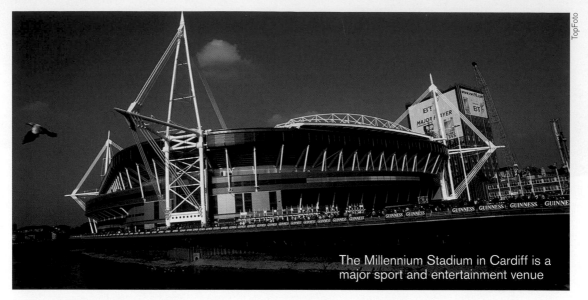

The Millennium Stadium in Cardiff is a major sport and entertainment venue

Examples of secondary purposes for major sports and entertainment venues (other than tours) are hosting:

- conferences and business meetings
- exhibitions and trade fairs
- social functions, such as weddings
- other leisure events, such as a rock concert at a football stadium, or indoor sporting event at an arena

In a nutshell

Major sports and entertainment venues are visitor attractions because customers go there to:
* watch the sport or entertainment that is the venue's main purpose
* see or tour the venue
* take advantage of a secondary purpose of the venue, such as attending an exhibition held there

Test yourself

1 What is meant by a venue's 'secondary purpose'?

2 Give three examples of leisure activities that are available at sports/entertainment venues.

Boost your grade Be ready to compare the UK and overseas sports and entertainment venues you have studied.

GCSE Revision Guide

Topic 14
Built attractions

What the specification requires

You need to be able to describe built attractions.

In brief

Built attractions are sites that were specifically constructed to attract leisure visitors and tourists. A cathedral is not a built attraction because it was built to be a place of worship. Cathedrals such as Durham Cathedral and York Minster became visitor attractions later. They are historic attractions. However, the purpose of museums and art galleries has always been as a visitor attraction, so they are built attractions.

Speak the language

built attraction — an attraction that was purpose-built to be a visitor attraction

Revision notes

Built attractions are visitor sites that were specifically constructed to attract visitors.

Examples from the UK include the London Eye and Spinnaker Tower in Portsmouth.

Public museums and art galleries are types of built attraction. Part of their purpose is to conserve old objects, documents and works of art but they have also been developed to display these to visitors. Examples include the British Museum and the National Gallery in London.

The American Museum of Natural History, New York City, USA is an overseas example of a built attraction. The museum has various halls including:

- Dinosaur Hall — the largest exhibition of dinosaur remains in the world with over 120 specimens on show
- Hall of Biodiversity — interactive and multimedia displays relating to the variety of nature
- Hall of North American Mammals — featuring stuffed creatures, including a pair of bull moose in fighting pose
- Hall of Planet Earth — a multimedia exhibition about how the Earth was formed and is constantly changing

The Hall of Planet Earth houses the Dynamic Earth Globe exhibit, which gives a view of the Earth as it rotates, as though from a satellite or orbiting spaceship. The Haydn Planetarium is attached to the museum and shows a three-dimensional film called *Passport to the Universe* inside a glass sphere that is more than 25 metres in diameter.

The American Museum of Natural History, New York

In a nutshell

Built attractions were deliberately built to attract visitors. Museums and art galleries are examples of built attractions because they were developed to attract visitors to view their exhibits.

Test yourself

1 What is meant by a 'built attraction'?

2 Outline the range of leisure activities available to visitors at the American Museum of Natural History.

Boost your grade Be clear about which attractions are built attractions and which are historic attractions. For example, the Tower of London is an historic attraction whereas Madame Tussaud's wax museum in London is a built attraction.

Topic 15
Transport in the UK

What the specification requires

You need to know the principal transport modes, routes, terminals and gateways used by people as they travel to, from and around the UK.

In brief

People use different forms of transport (air, rail, road, sea) to move around the UK. Leisure customers often travel locally, tourists make longer journeys. Journeys involve choices such as which route to take. Aircraft, trains, coaches and ferries all begin and end their journeys at **terminals** (airports, principal railway stations, coach stations and ports). UK **gateways** are those airports, principal railway stations, coach stations and ports by which travellers enter or leave the country.

Revision notes

People must travel to reach leisure and tourism destinations and attractions. Their trips range from short local hops, perhaps to visit the nearby leisure centre, to international journeys to and from overseas destinations, for example for a holiday in a beach or seaside resort abroad.

People travel to destinations in different ways. They can use different forms (modes) of transport, different routes or different **transport providers**.

Various **modes of transport** that people use to reach leisure and tourism destinations are:
- rail transport (trains, trams and **metro systems**)
- road transport (cars, buses and coaches, taxis and cycles)
- water transport (ferries and other ships and boats)
- air transport

Sometimes people can choose between different routes even if they are using the same mode of transport. For example, a traveller driving her/his own car (or one they have hired) may be able to choose between a short, direct route through a town and the by-pass, which may be longer in distance but quicker in time. On other occasions, the mode of transport chosen for a particular journey may decide the route. For example, a rail passenger between London and Paris has no choice but to travel through the Channel Tunnel.

Even for the same mode of transport on the same route, there may be a choice of provider. For example, a tourist travelling between London and Paris by air will have a choice of several airlines — both **flag-carrier airlines** and **budget carriers**.

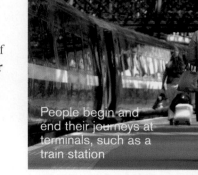

People begin and end their journeys at terminals, such as a train station

Sources of information about ways to travel to leisure and tourism destinations include:

- timetables
- atlases and route maps
- travel providers and online travel companies, including their internet sites
- destination information providers such as tourism information centres
- leisure facility and visitor attractions and their promotional materials, including websites
- travel guides: books and internet sites

The Channel Tunnel is 50 km long. It connects Folkestone in Kent to Coquelles in northern France. The Channel Tunnel was bored through the rocks that lie beneath the sea bed of the English Channel. It is really three tunnels in one:

- northbound tunnel (France to the UK)
- southbound tunnel (the UK to France)
- service tunnel

Eurotunnel shuttle trains carrying tourists and their cars, and Eurostar trains carrying passengers operate through the Channel Tunnel, taking people to their leisure and tourism destinations.

Speak the language

terminal — one end of a transport link. For example, terminal railway stations such as Waterloo, Kings Cross and Paddington are all at the London end of railway lines leading to other parts of the UK

gateway — a point of entry into a country. For example, New York's John F. Kennedy Airport is a gateway airport for people entering and leaving the USA

transport provider — a leisure and tourism organisation that operates travel services

mode of transport — a form of transport: rail and air are examples

metro system — an urban light railway network. Many large cities in the UK (such as London, Newcastle upon Tyne and Manchester) and overseas (such as Paris, New York and Milan) have metros. Sometimes, as in the case of the London Underground, these are largely beneath the surface

flag-carrier airline — an air transport provider that represents its home country around the world and is not a budget airline. Examples include British Airways and Air France

budget carrier — an air transport provider that carries people at discounted fares. Budget airlines operate more basic, sometimes called no-frills, services than flag-carrier airlines

In a nutshell

The journeys people make to leisure and tourism destinations can be simple or more complex. A tourist's journey from home to a hotel in an overseas holiday destination may involve a number of stages, modes, routes and providers.

Test yourself

1 Give four different types of transport mode.

2 Choose one UK leisure and tourism destination. Give two different ways in which visitors can travel there.

3 What are:
   (a) gateways?
   (b) terminals?

Boost your grade

People travel to leisure and tourism destinations in various ways. These include different:
- modes
- routes
- transport providers

Any one journey may involve several of each. Talk to people about journeys they have made to collect some examples.

Topic 16
Travel to leisure and tourism destinations

What the specification requires

You need to understand that people can choose to travel to leisure and tourism destinations using different forms of transport. They can pick different routes and transport providers, and can often choose different prices.

In brief

A journey from home to a leisure and tourism destination can involve several different stages, perhaps using different transport modes. On the other hand, a simple door-to-door cycle or car journey may be all that is needed. This is particularly true for a local trip or to a domestic leisure and tourism destination.

Multi-stage trips may be long-distance, such as to an overseas leisure and tourism destination, or they may simply be across a city. A long trip does not necessarily mean more stages. For example, the journey made by a package holiday-maker from a suburban housing estate to a long-haul beach destination such as Phuket in Thailand is likely to involve the same number of stages as a journey to a short-haul seaside resort such as Palma Nova in Mallorca.

An independent traveller is likely to investigate travel options using the internet. Surfing the websites of transport providers such as airlines, train-operating companies, ferry operators and car-hire firms allows people to compare and evaluate their options without leaving their home. Online travel companies such as Expedia and Opodo allow easy comparison of a range (but not all) of different providers.

Using online travel companies allows people to compare transport options

Revision notes

A trip from Glasgow to London is one example of a journey that could be taken by a business tourist.

Business tourists wanting to travel from Glasgow to London have a variety of options open to them. Three possible transport modes are:

- air — scheduled flights operate from Glasgow Airport to London's airports
- rail — train operators Virgin Trains and National Express run express trains between Glasgow and London's Euston and Kings Cross railway station terminals
- road — via the UK's trunk road and motorway system

There are advantages and disadvantages to each mode relating to journey time, convenience and comfort, price and environmental impact.

Speak the language

Transport for London — the public sector organisation that oversees the provision of public transport in London

Traveline — a partnership of transport providers and local councils providing information about public transport in the UK

In a nutshell

People travelling to leisure and tourism destinations choose among different travel options:
* modes and facilities
* routes
* providers
* prices

Modes of transport include rail, road, water and air transport.

Transport facilities that may act as transport terminals or gateways include railway stations, ferry ports and airports.

Transport providers are leisure and tourism organisations that include:
* train-operating companies
* car-hire firms
* ferry operators
* airlines

Sources you can use to find out about travel from your home area to leisure and tourism destinations include:
* the websites of transport providers, online travel companies and travel information services provided by organisations such as the AA (Automobile Association), **Transport for London** and **Traveline**
* road and travel atlases, maps
* travel guidebooks
* transport timetables
* tour operator brochures

Think through the advantages and disadvantages of various travel options to leisure and tourism destinations for different types of customer.

There are different categories of tourists, one example is business tourists. For each category, try to think of the types of traveller the category will include. For example, business tourists are likely to include:
- single travellers
- groups of colleagues travelling together
- people of different adult age groups
- different ethnic and cultural groups
- people with special needs

Remember that, other than for business, the main purposes of tourism are:
- leisure
- to visit friends and relatives

Test yourself

1 When deciding how to travel to a leisure and tourism destination people can choose among different transport providers. Give three other transport choices they need to make.

2 Compare the advantages and disadvantages to a business tourist of travelling from Glasgow to London by air with those of travelling by rail.

3 How suitable do you think the option of travelling by road would be for a business tourist. Why?

Topic 17
Tourism impacts

What the specification requires

You need to understand and be able to explain economic, social and environmental impacts on destinations, local communities and globally.

In brief

When tourists visit a destination they have an effect on it. They affect its environment and they affect the local community who live there. The effects that tourists have are **tourism's impact**. Some effects are good for the environment or good for the local people. These benefits are the **positive impacts** of tourism. Other effects of tourism are **negative impacts**. Negative impacts are damaging to the destination's economy, to its society or to the environment.

The people who live in leisure and tourism destinations make up its **host community**. Members of the host community benefit economically from tourism because it provides:

- jobs
- money

Revision notes

Impacts of tourism can be classified as:

- **economic impacts**, which affect jobs and money in destinations
- **social impacts**, which affect people themselves, their way of life and what facilities are available for them
- **environmental impacts**, which affect not only the nature of the destination itself but the global environment as well

Tourists spend money. They are customers of the local leisure and tourism organisations in a destination, making use of the facilities these organisations provide. Such facilities include visitor

Tourism has positive and negative impacts on the host community

Leslie Derek Sanders/Fotolia

attractions, cafés, bars, restaurants, entertainment venues, hotels, amusements and local transport. In a seaside resort, for example, there will be many such facilities, all requiring people to operate them, and so large numbers of jobs are created. This is a positive economic impact of tourism on the local, host community.

The money spent by tourists on facilities allows leisure and tourism and other businesses to prosper and grow, perhaps creating more jobs. Job-holders are paid wages, which they spend in other businesses in and around the destination and pay tax on them to the local government.

However, there are disadvantages:
- jobs may only be seasonal
- some money leaks away

Many seaside resorts experience seasonal variations in **tourism flow**. The number of visitors is likely to be high in the summer months (the **peak or high season**), less in spring and autumn (sometimes called the **shoulder season**) and low in the out-of-season winter months (**low season**). As a result many of the jobs generated by tourism are seasonal and job-holders find themselves unemployed in the winter. This is particularly the case for UK seaside and beach resorts. In destinations such as Scarborough and Blackpool, the local council and leisure and tourism organisations encourage business tourism to generate a higher low-season tourism flow.

Some leisure and tourism businesses in a destination are not locally owned. Hotels and bar and restaurant **chains**, for example, are often owned by organisations based elsewhere (often in another country). The profits made by such facilities are taken away from the destination and taxes paid on them are collected elsewhere. This effect is called **economic leakage**. Like seasonal unemployment, it is a negative economic impact of tourism.

Speak the language

tourism's impact — the effects that tourism has on the environment and on people who live in destinations

positive impact — the benefits that tourism brings

negative impact — the harm that tourism causes

host community — the local population of a tourist destination

economic impact — the effect of tourism on employment, and on income and standards of living in destinations

social impact — the effect of tourism on the way of life of people who live in destinations

environmental impact — the effect of tourism on the quality of the environment both in destinations and elsewhere as result of travel (for example the impact of air travel on the atmosphere)

tourism flow — the number of tourists who travel to a destination. It often varies seasonally

peak or high season — the busiest period of the year for a leisure and tourism destination. Tourism flow is high

shoulder season — tourism flows are at an intermediate level in this period, either side of the high or peak season

low season — a quiet period of the year when few tourists visit a destination

chain — a business, such as a leisure and tourism organisation, which has a number of branches or outlets in different locations. The Sandals hotel chain is one example

economic leakage — money which is spent in a destination but is lost to another location

In a nutshell

Tourism's impacts are the effects tourism has on the environment and on people who live in destinations.

Positive impacts are beneficial effects. Negative impacts are harmful effects.

Tourism's impacts can be classified as economic, social or environmental.

Boost your grade

Tourism is often seasonal. Seaside resorts in the UK and some overseas locations (such as around the Mediterranean Sea) attract most tourists in the summer. This is when the weather is most likely to be warm and sunny. The summer is the peak season (the busiest time). At other times of year there are fewer tourists. In the winter, a UK seaside destination may have hardly any tourists at all. Some facilities may close for a few weeks. Such a quiet period is out of season.

Think beyond the simple and obvious:
- Don't just think tourism brings jobs, but what jobs and when?
- Don't just think individual tourists can be noisy and drop litter.
- Think about the wider impacts of tourism.

Test yourself

1 Give three types of impact that tourism can have.

2 What is the difference between positive and negative impacts?

Topic 18
Sustainability, responsible tourism and ecotourism

What the specification requires

You need to understand and be able to explain the meanings of sustainability, responsible tourism and ecotourism.

In brief

Sustainability in leisure and tourism means operating facilities and managing activities so that they have minimal negative impact on the environment and people's ways of life.

Sustainability is very important to leisure and tourism, not just in the UK but also internationally. Sustainability in leisure and tourism is about customers and organisations behaving in ways that do not damage the environment or harm the communities who live in leisure and tourism destinations.

Frantisek Hojdysz/Fotolia

Ecotourists try to limit their effect on the natural environment

Responsible tourism is visiting destinations in ways that negatively affect the environment and local people as little as possible. Tourism that is responsible is therefore sustainable. Responsible tourists act in ways that maximise the positive impact of tourism. For example, UK visitors to long-haul destinations in the Less Economically Developed World (LEDW) can act responsibly by buying products and services directly from local people. In this way the economic benefit of tourism goes directly to members of the host community.

Ecotourism is visiting a leisure and tourism destination because of the appeal of its natural environment while negatively affecting the environment as little as possible. Ecotourism is normally tourism on a small scale because mass tourism is likely to affect a destination's natural environment. Ecotourists try to be responsible tourists and to benefit the local communities they visit socially and economically.

Revision notes

Sustainable development in the leisure and tourism industry is about making changes that improve activities and facilities for customers in ways that minimise negative impacts. This means in ways that protect the environment and local people's ways of life for the future.

Behaving sustainably minimises the negative impacts of leisure and tourism. It helps to protect the future of the environment and of destinations and their people. This is important for the economic future of destinations. People will not want to visit places that have been spoilt by the negative impact of tourism in the past.

Changes in UK leisure and tourism destinations, such as the development of new visitor attractions, cause tourism impacts. It is important that developments are managed sustainably to protect the future of the environment and the local community.

Sustainability matters in overseas destinations as well as those in the UK. Sustainability matters to:
- local people
- tourists
- leisure and tourism organisations

Sustainable tourism developments minimise negative impacts on the environment so that destinations remain pleasant places to live and work, as well as to visit. Destinations that are developed sustainably will have sufficient resources in the future for the continuation of local life and tourism.

Speak the language

sustainability — the ability to sustain or conserve the environment and people's ways of life into the future by minimising negative impacts, for example of tourism development

responsible tourism — leisure and tourism organisations or individual tourists behaving in ways that maximise the positive and minimise the negative impacts of tourism

ecotourism — visiting a destination to enjoy its natural environment without damaging it

sustainable development — growth, for example of leisure and tourism, that is planned to minimise negative impact on the environment and on people's lives

eco-lodge — a small hotel or guest-house that is run to ecotourism principles

guest-house — a small hotel with limited facilities that concentrates on providing accommodation and meals

renewable energy — sources of power that are replaced naturally, such as solar, wind and water power

In recent years tourists have become increasingly aware of the potential negative impacts of their travel. Many want to play their part in keeping negative impacts as low as possible. Leisure and tourism organisations including airlines, hotel accommodation providers and tour operators are aware of this. As a result they promote sustainable leisure and tourism products/services.

The aims of ecotourism are:
- to help people enjoy and learn about the natural environment in leisure and tourism destinations
- to conserve the natural environment of leisure and tourism destinations by minimising the negative environmental impacts of tourism
- to make positive impacts, not only on the environment but also on the lives and well-being of local people

An eco-lodge in a safari park in Kenya

Eco-lodges are small-scale ecotourism hotels or **guest-houses**. Typically, eco-lodges are owned and run by individuals. Owners make real efforts to protect the environment by conserving natural resources and limiting waste. They do this by:
- using cooler water for laundry
- changing sheets and towels less frequently
- using solar power or another source of **renewable energy**
- having low-flow showerheads and toilets with reduced flushes
- buying recycled products and recycling their waste
- building a compost heap for kitchen and garden waste

Eco-lodges are also sustainable because their owners benefit the local community economically and socially by buying food from local producers and by employing local staff.

In a nutshell

Sustainable development involves minimising negative impacts so that what happens now does not significantly harm the environment and people of the future. It may not be possible to reduce negative impacts to zero. However, ensuring that they are slight has increasingly been considered possible in recent years. Will this be enough to protect the future?

Responsible tourism is about behaviour. Leisure and tourism organisations and individual tourists can choose to behave responsibly by trying to have:
* the maximum possible positive impact, and
* the minimum possible negative impact
on host communities and on the environment.

Ecotourism is visiting a destination to enjoy its natural environment without spoiling it. Ecotourism is small-scale tourism, not mass tourism. Ecotourists want to benefit the local community economically without upsetting their traditional way of life.

Test yourself

1 Explain what is meant by
   (a) 'sustainability'
   (b) 'responsible tourism'

2 Explain why sustainability matters.

3 Give two aims of sustainable development.

4 What is meant by:
   (a) 'eco-lodge'?
   (b) 'mass tourism'?

5 Why is mass tourism not ecotourism?

Boost your grade
You need to be able to explain clearly what sustainability is and why it is increasingly thought to be important. Work out what you would say before you sit the examination.

Be clear about the meanings of:
■ sustainable
■ responsible
■ ecotourism

How are they the same? How are they different?

1 Name one long-haul city destination. *(1 mark)*

2 Name a UK beach (or seaside) resort you have studied and identify one of its attractions. *(2 marks)*

3 Choose one ski/snowsports resort. Explain how it meets the needs of people of different ages. *(6 marks)*

4 Give two factors that affect people's choices of leisure and tourism destinations. Explain how they may affect a retired couple deciding on an overseas destination for a holiday. *(6 marks)*

5 Give one UK and one overseas example of each of the following:
   (a) historic attraction
   (b) built attraction
   (c) natural attraction *(6 marks)*

6 Outline the difference between a built attraction and a historic site. *(2 marks)*

7 Explain how one visitor attraction meets the needs of one of these types of leisure and tourism customer:
   ■ couples
   ■ groups
   ■ people of different ages *(6 marks)*

8 Which one of the following statements is true?
   ■ Eurostar trains operate to and from Paris.
   ■ Piccadilly is a major London airport.
   ■ Virgin Trains operates trains on the East Coast main line. *(1 mark)*

9 Two university students want to travel from your local area to an overseas city destination that you have studied. Discuss their travel options. *(9 marks)*

10 Give three modes of transport. *(3 marks)*

11 Give two examples of London railway terminals. *(2 marks)*

12 Name three UK airports other than London airports. *(3 marks)*

13 Outline the difference between public transport and private transport. *(2 marks)*

14 What is an online travel service? *(2 marks)*

15 Outline one way that tourism can have a negative impact on a destination. *(2 marks)*

16 What is ecotourism? *(2 marks)*

17 A family of two adults and their teenage daughter want an ecotourism holiday in a destination you have studied. Suggest where they should go and how they should behave as responsible tourists while they are there. Justify your suggestions. *(9 marks)*

18 Give one example of how tourism can have each of the following impacts:

   (a) (i) positive economic

       (ii) negative economic

   (b) (i) positive social

       (ii) negative social

   (c) (i) positive environmental

       (ii) negative environmental   *(6 marks)*

19 What is meant by each of these:

   (a) sustainability?

   (b) responsible tourism?   *(4 marks)*

20 Study Figure 1. Complete the key by matching the national leisure facilities shown with the correct location letters. Beamish Museum has been done for you as an example.   *(8 marks)*

Figure 1

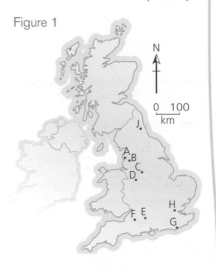

Key

Facility		Location
Museums and galleries	Beamish Museum	J
	Ironbridge Gorge	
	The National Gallery	
Visitor attractions	Blackpool Tower and Pleasure Beach	
	Longleat Safari Park	
	Place Pier, Brighton	
Theme park	Camelot	
Historic sites	Chatsworth	
	Stonehenge	

21 Study Figure 2. Suggest two activities at Ironbridge Gorge that would appeal to the young children in a family.   *(2 marks)*

22 Describe the location and purpose of one UK built attraction such as a museum or art gallery.   *(4 marks)*

Figure 2

23 On Figure 3 draw six arrows to link each named UK attraction with one true statement about it. Beamish has been done for you as an example. *(6 marks)*

Figure 3

Beamish	The Crown Jewels are a major attraction here
The Royal Armouries	Where a ride is called a flight
The London Eye	A waxwork museum in central London
Madame Tussaud's	A theme park based on the story of King Arthur
Camelot	Out of London, by the River Thames, and famous for its maze
Hampton Court Palace	An open-air museum in Northeast England
Tower of London	Situated in Leeds

24 Choose one of the UK attractions listed in Figure 2. Evaluate how suitable it would be for a family of two adults and two children aged 5 and 13 years to visit. *(8 marks)*

25 Explain the relative merits of travel:
  (a) by sea and air from Northern Ireland to London
  (b) by rail and road between the North of England and London *(6 marks)*

26 Figure 4 shows a countryside area in Devon. Suggest three reasons why countryside destinations are popular with visitors. *(3 marks)*

Figure 4

27 Study Figure 5.
  (a) Label National Parks Dartmoor and Exmoor. *(2 marks)*
  (b) Describe the location of Dartmoor. *(2 marks)*
  (c) Suggest two qualities of an area that might lead it to be designated a National Park. *(2 marks)*

Figure 5

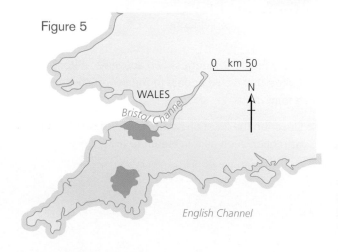

WALES

Bristol Channel

0   km 50

N

English Channel

28 The scrambled names of five UK seaside towns/cities are shown below. Unscramble each name and write it next to the appropriate statement in the table.

koplacbol   benty   olddannul   nibthorg   thurspro

This Sussex resort is home to the Palace Pier.

On the Fylde coast of Lancashire and famous for its Golden Mile.

On the Pembrokeshire coast of South Wales.

Near to the Giant's Causeway — a visitor attraction in County Antrim.

A North Wales resort with two bays, either side of the Great Orme.

(5 marks)

29 Figure 6 shows tourism amenities and facilities in the seaside town of Scarborough.
   (a) Use Figure 6 to complete the table below with two examples of facilities in each of the attractions and accommodation and catering sections. *(5 marks)*
   (b) Compare what Scarborough and one other UK seaside town offer their visitors. *(4 marks)*

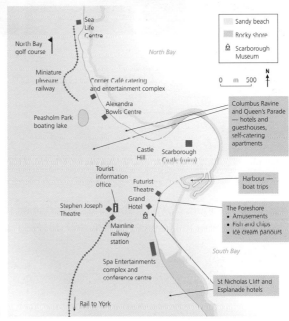

Figure 6

Attractions	Tourist information and guiding services
	Tourist information office

Transportation	Accommodation and catering
Mainline railway station	

30 (a) Figure 7 shows historic and built attractions in four tourist towns/cities in the UK. Put the name of each sight and its city in the table below. *(4 marks)*

Figure 7

Photograph	Sight	City
(a)		
(b)		
(c)		
(d)		

(b) Use Figure 8, which shows transport links to the tourist city of Edinburgh, to help you reply to the email in Figure 9. *(4 marks)*

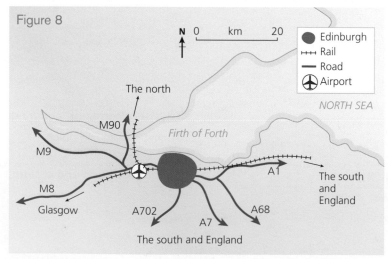

Figure 9 An email enquiry for Edinburgh tourist information

To: info@visitscotland.com

Hello

I am planning to visit Edinburgh but am unsure how I will travel. I live in London. Please can you advise me of the alternatives.

Thank you

Ms Claire Knight

31 Study Figure 10 which gives information about some tourism impacts in a countryside tourism destination.

Figure 10

(a) Give two economic impacts (one positive and one negative) *(2 marks)*

(b) Outline two social impacts. *(2 marks)*

(c) Outline likely positive and negative environmental impacts. *(4 marks)*

32 (a) What is meant by sustainable development of tourism destinations? *(2 marks)*

(b) Suggest how destinations such as that shown in Figure 10 could be developed sustainably. *(3 marks)*

33 Use your knowledge of tourism destinations and methods of travel to design a three-day short break coach holiday in one area of the UK. *(6 marks)*

34 A South African couple are visiting friends who live in your local area.

(a) They want to entertain their hosts' two children (aged 9 and 14 years) to a day of leisure activities as a thank you. Use your knowledge of local leisure facilities to plan their day. *(3 marks)*

(b) The South African couple plan to spend a week touring the UK on their own. Use your knowledge of tourism destinations and transport in the UK to suggest and justify a programme for them. *(9 marks)*

Unit 2
The nature of leisure and tourism

Controlled assessment

Controlled assessment describes how your coursework project for Unit 2 (and also for Unit 4 if you are taking the Double Award) is set up, run and marked.

Controlled assessment is very important in GCSE Leisure and Tourism because it is worth 60% of your total final marks — whether you are sitting GCSE Leisure and Tourism or GCSE Leisure and Tourism (Double Award). It is sensible therefore to spend 60% of the course time on the controlled assessment unit(s); this includes both lessons and project(s).

Examples of controlled assessment tasks can be found on pages 69 and 124.

Key stages

There are three key stages in the controlled assessment process:
1 task setting — when you are set your project task
2 task taking — when you do the work to complete your set task
3 task marking — when your work is marked

What happens in each of these stages?

1 Task setting

AQA sets a choice of three tasks. You and/or your teacher will choose which one of these you will do. You may do the same one as everybody else in your class or you may not, but your task must be one of the three set by AQA. Your teacher will help you set your work in the context of your centre — for Unit 2 this often relates to the leisure and tourism industry locally or to a visit you have made to a particular leisure and tourism organisation.

For GCSE Leisure and Tourism and GCSE Leisure and Tourism (Double Award), AQA sets controlled assessment tasks every 2 years. They are published in advance on AQA's website.

Each task requires you to:
- analyse issue(s)/problem(s)
- decide what information to collect and then collect it
- demonstrate your knowledge and understanding using written communication
- analyse and evaluate evidence
- make reasoned judgements
- present conclusions

Tasks are divided into parts, called strands. Each strand addresses one of the criteria used to assess your work. There are six assessment criteria for each controlled assessment unit. The strands cover all three Assessment Objectives (AO) of the course. Assessment Objectives describe what you should be able to do when you have finished your course. In the context of the controlled assessment units they are:
- AO1 — select and communicate knowledge and understanding.
- AO2 — apply skills, knowledge and understanding in planning and carrying out investigations and tasks.
- AO3 — analyse and evaluate information, sources and evidence, make reasoned judgements and present conclusions.

2 Task taking

You will have some lessons about the unit before you begin to do the task itself. You might go on a visit or a speaker may visit your centre. You should make sure that you know and understand the assessment criteria for the unit before you start. You will be marked according to how well you have completed each assessment criterion. The assessment criteria for Unit 2 are explained below. Those for Unit 4 are explained later in the book.

Your project task for Unit 2 should take you about 45 hours to complete. This includes preparation time (going on a visit, for example) but not lesson time spent on learning about the unit's content. This is a guideline figure only. It is a good idea to spend equal amounts of time on each of the six assessment criteria for Unit 2. It is also a good idea to complete one assessment criterion at a time, writing each up as you go, rather than waiting until the end and having to do them all at once.

Most students use a word processor for their work, but it is not necessary. Handwritten work is perfectly acceptable.

Your research will be done under 'limited supervision'. Limited supervision means that your teacher will keep an eye on what you are doing but you can collect information independently. You can do that in small groups, providing each group member's role is clear and you can demonstrate that you took an active part.

Once you have done your research, you will be under 'informal supervision'. Informal supervision means that you do not have to write up your work under examination conditions but it also means that your teacher will check that:
- you have not plagiarised your work (for example, copied it from someone else, from a book or copied and pasted unacknowledged sections of websites)
- you have clearly recorded the sources you have chosen and used
- your work is your own
- you have completed the task as set by AQA

Your teacher can give you guidance while you are writing up your work, but this will be limited. Your teacher can advise you how to approach your work, check it and can give you general feedback, but cannot tell you exactly how to rewrite bits to score higher marks. Any guidance your teacher does give you has to be recorded on the front sheet (Candidate Record Form) of your work and sent to AQA. Your teacher can tell you how well you are doing and suggest general ways to improve but cannot give you detailed corrections and suggestions. That would be breaking the rules.

While you are doing your research, you should keep notes to help you in writing up your work. It is good to include primary and secondary sources of information.

- Primary sources are those you have used to gather information yourself, for example by using questionnaires, surveys, interviews or observation.
- Secondary sources are those you have used to look up information collected by others. They include promotional materials, books, maps and websites.

You must clearly reference all sources you have used. A bibliography is a good idea.

Your research notes will be kept by your teacher and sent to AQA if requested.

3 Task marking

Your teacher will mark your work. The assessment criteria will be used to decide what score your teacher thinks you should have (not what grade). AQA will check your teacher's marking to make sure that every student is treated the same, no matter which teacher they had. This is called moderation. AQA will decide on the grade for your work.

Assessment criteria

Strand A

Strand A is about planning and carrying out your investigation.

As for all strands, Strand A is assessed against three levels of quality. Your teacher will score your finished work within one of these three levels.

Level 1 (up to 4 marks)

To gain a Level 1 score for Strand A you should outline how you went about collecting and recording your evidence.

You should also:
Give reasons why you went about it the way you did.

Level 2 (5 to 9 marks)

At this level, you will:
- clearly identify the evidence that you have collected
- clearly describe (in sentences and paragraphs, *not* lists and bullet points) how you collected your evidence and how you recorded it

You should also:
Clearly explain (in sentences and paragraphs, *not* lists and bullet points) why you used the methods you did.

Level 3 (10 to 14 marks)

At this level, you will:

- clearly identify the evidence that you have collected, and
- describe in detail (as fully as you can, in sentences and paragraphs) how you collected your evidence and how you recorded it

You should also:

Fully justify the methods you used (explain in detail why they were the correct/best methods, in sentences and paragraphs).

To get the maximum marks in Strand A:

- make sure you understand exactly what you are doing and why you are doing it
- keep a careful record of all the information you collect, including when and where you found it
- if you are working in a group, take a full and active part
- include examples of data collecting sheets (not every one — just examples) in your finished work
- do not write up all of this strand immediately — it will be easier to give reasons for/explain/justify your methods when you see the outcome of your research
- so, finish writing up Strand A at the end

Strand B

The second strand for Unit 2 is about how people use leisure and tourism facilities provided in a place or by a leisure and tourism organisation, depending on which task option you have chosen.

You might prefer to do the work for Strand B *after* you have done Strand C. This is because Strand C is about what the facilities are. You might think it is logical to deal with that before describing how people use them.

However, do not try to do the two strands together. It doesn't work! Do one strand, then the other, and write up each completely independently within separate sections of your finished project.

As for all strands, Strand B is assessed against three levels of quality. Your teacher will score your finished work within one of these three levels.

Level 1 (up to 4 marks)

To gain a Level 1 score for Strand B you need to describe (using sentences, *not* bullet points) how people use leisure and tourism facilities that are provided in a place or by a leisure and tourism organisation.

Level 2 (5 to 8 marks)

At Level 2, you will need to describe *clearly* (using sentences and paragraphs, *not* bullet points) how people use *some* leisure and tourism facilities provided in a place or by a leisure and tourism organisation.

Level 3 (9 to 12 marks)

At Level 3, you will need to describe *in detail* (using full sentences and paragraphs) how people use a *variety* of leisure and tourism facilities provided in a place or by a leisure and tourism organisation.

To get the maximum marks in Strand B:

- do Strand C first!
- make sure you understand exactly what you are doing

- always write in sentences and paragraphs, avoid the temptation to produce bullet point lists
- if you are working in a group, make sure you take a full and active part
- include a representative range of the facilities provided in the place or by the leisure and tourism organisation you are investigating. Try to include *examples* of all the facilities that people use.

Strand C

Strand C is about the range of leisure and tourism facilities currently provided in a place or by a leisure and tourism organisation (Strand D is about recent changes), depending on which task option you have chosen.

You may prefer to do the work for Strand C *before* you do Strand B. This is because Strand C is about what the facilities are. You might think it is logical to deal with that before describing how people use them in Strand B.

However, do not try to do the two strands together. It doesn't work! Do one strand, then the other, and write up each completely independently within separate sections of your finished project.

As for all strands, Strand C is assessed against three levels of quality. Your teacher will score your finished work within one of these three levels.

Level 1 (up to 4 marks)

To gain a Level 1 score for Strand C you need to describe (using sentences, *not* bullet points) *some* leisure and tourism facilities that are currently provided in a place or by a leisure and tourism organisation.

You should also:
Give reasons why these facilities are provided in that place or by the organisation concerned.

Level 2 (5 to 9 marks)

At Level 2, you will need to describe (clearly, using sentences and paragraphs, *not* bullet points) the *range* of leisure and tourism facilities that are currently provided in a place or by a leisure and tourism organisation.

You should also:
- clearly explain (in sentences and paragraphs) why these facilities are provided in the place of by the organisation concerned
- draw some conclusions about what facilities are provided and why

Level 3 (10 to 14 marks)

To be awarded Level 3, you will need to describe *in detail* (using full sentences and paragraphs) **and** *account for* (fully explain reasons for) the *range* of leisure and tourism facilities that are currently provided in a place or by a leisure and tourism organisation.

You should also:
- draw valid conclusions about what facilities are provided and why
- justify your conclusions (fully)

To get the maximum marks in Strand C:
- do Strand C before Strand B!
- make sure you understand exactly what you are doing
- always write in sentences and paragraphs, avoid the temptation to produce bullet point lists

- if you are working in a group, make sure you take a full and active part
- describe and exemplify the full range of facilities provided in the place or by the leisure and tourism organisation you are investigating. Try to include *examples* of all the types of facilities that people use.

Strand D

Strand D is about recent changes in leisure and tourism in a place or leisure and tourism organisation, depending on which task option you have chosen.

Recent changes are taken to be those of approximately the last 20 years.

Do the work for Strand C *before* you do Strand D. This is because Strand C is about current facilities. It is logical to know about current facilities before describing the recent changes required by Strand D.

However, do not try to do the two strands together. It doesn't work! Do one strand, then the other, and write up each completely independently within separate sections of your finished project.

As for all strands, Strand D is assessed against three levels of quality. Your teacher will score your finished work within one of these three levels.

Level 1 (up to 4 marks)

To gain a Level 1 score for Strand D you need to describe (using sentences, *not* bullet points) *some* recent changes in leisure and tourism in a place or by a leisure and tourism organisation.

Level 2 (5 to 9 marks)

At Level 2, you will need to describe *clearly* (using sentences and paragraphs, *not* bullet points) *some* recent changes in leisure and tourism in a place or by a leisure and tourism organisation.

You should also:

- provide some explanation (use sentences and paragraphs) of why these changes have happened or are happening now
- draw some conclusions about what changes have happened or are happening now, and why

Level 3 (10 to 14 marks)

To be awarded Level 3, you will need to analyse *in detail* (using full sentences and paragraphs) a *variety* of recent changes in leisure and tourism in a place or by a leisure and tourism organisation.

You should also:

- draw conclusions about what facilities are provided and why
- justify your conclusions (fully)

To get the maximum marks in Strand D:

- do it after Strands C and B (in that order!)
- make sure you understand exactly what you are doing
- always write in sentences and paragraphs, avoid the temptation to produce bullet point lists
- if you are working in a group, make sure you take a full and active part
- describe and exemplify the full range of facilities provided in the place or by the leisure and tourism organisation you are investigating. Try to include *examples* of changes in all the types of facilities that people use.

Strand E

Strand E is about the range of promotional materials and techniques used by one leisure and tourism organisation in the place you are investigating for your project, or by the leisure and tourism organisation you are investigating for your project. It depends on which task option you have chosen.

It is a good idea to complete the work for Strands B, C and D *before* you do Strand E. This is because Strands B, C and D are all about facilities: what they currently are, who uses them and how they have changed. It is logical to know about them before describing the use of promotional materials and techniques, as required by Strand E.

However, do not try to do two or more strands together. It doesn't work! Do one strand, then another, and write up each completely independently within separate sections of your finished project.

As for all strands, Strand E is assessed against three levels of quality. Your teacher will score your finished work within one of these three levels.

However, you also need to be aware that Strand E is used to assess the quality of your written communication (how well you use written English to demonstrate your knowledge and understanding). Of course, you should always use your best English, but it is especially important that you do so here.

Level 1 (up to 4 marks)

To gain a Level 1 score for Strand E you need to describe (using sentences, *not* bullet points) *some* promotional materials and techniques used by one leisure and tourism organisation in the place you are investigating for your project or by the leisure and tourism organisation you are investigating for your project.

You should also:
- use *some* specialist leisure and tourism terms that you have learned from your course
- write legibly, so people can read your work easily
- use your best spelling and grammar, and check both

Level 2 (5 to 9 marks)

At Level 2, you will need to describe *clearly* (using sentences and paragraphs, *not* bullet points) *some* promotional materials and techniques used by one leisure and tourism organisation in the place you are investigating for your project or by the leisure and tourism organisation you are investigating for your project.

You should also:
- evaluate promotional materials *and/or* techniques used
- use a *good range* of specialist leisure and tourism terms that you have learned from your course
- write legibly, so people can read your work easily
- use your best spelling and grammar, and check both

Level 3 (10 to 14 marks)

At Level 3, you will need to analyse *in detail* (using full sentences and paragraphs) a *variety* of promotional materials and techniques used by one leisure and tourism organisation in the place you are investigating for your project or by the leisure and tourism organisation you are investigating for your project.

You should also:
- evaluate *in detail* a *variety* of promotional materials *and* techniques used
- use a *wide range* of specialist leisure and tourism terms that you have learned from your course
- write legibly, so people can read your work easily
- use your best spelling and grammar, and check both

To get the maximum marks in Strand E:
- do it after Strands C, B and D (Strand C first)
- make sure you understand exactly what you are doing
- always write in sentences and paragraphs, avoid the temptation to produce bullet point lists
- if you are working in a group, make sure you take a full and active part
- describe a full range of promotional materials and techniques that are actually used by one leisure and tourism organisation in the place you are investigating for your project or by the leisure and tourism organisation you are investigating for your project.

Strand F

Strand F is the sixth strand for Unit 2. Depending on the order in which you have done the others, it might be the last one. Strand F is about the range of leisure and tourism employment opportunities available for young people in a place or in a leisure and tourism organisation, depending on which task option you have chosen.

The term 'young people' means people who have recently left school/college/university and are therefore in their late teens or twenties.

It is a good idea to complete the work for Strands B, C and D *before* you do Strand F. This is because Strands B, C and D are all about facilities: what they currently are, who uses them and how they have changed. It is logical to know about them before describing the range of leisure and tourism employment opportunities available for young people in a place or in a leisure and tourism organisation, as required by Strand F.

It does not matter whether you do Strand E before Strand F, or the other way around.

However, do not try to do two or more strands together. It doesn't work! Do one strand, then another, and write up each completely independently within separate sections of your finished project.

As for all strands, Strand F is assessed against three levels of quality. Your teacher will score your finished work within one of these three levels.

Level 1 (up to 4 marks)

To gain a Level 1 score for Strand F you need to describe (using sentences, *not* bullet points) a *range* of leisure and tourism employment opportunities available for young people in a place or in a leisure and tourism organisation.

Level 2 (5 to 8 marks)

At Level 2, you will need to describe *clearly* (using sentences and paragraphs, *not* bullet points) *some* leisure and tourism employment opportunities available for young people in a place or in a leisure and tourism organisation.

You should also:
Evaluate the range of leisure and tourism employment opportunities available for young people in a place or in a leisure and tourism organisation

Level 3 (9 to 12 marks)

At Level 3, you will need to describe *in detail* (using full sentences and paragraphs) a *range* of leisure and tourism employment opportunities available for young people in a place or in a leisure and tourism organisation.

You should also:

Evaluate *in detail* the *range* of leisure and tourism employment opportunities available for young people in a place or in a leisure and tourism organisation

To get the maximum marks in Strand F:

- do it after Strands C, B and D (Strand C first). It does not matter whether you do it before or after Strand E
- make sure you understand exactly what you are doing
- always write in sentences and paragraphs, avoid the temptation to produce bullet point lists
- if you are working in a group, make sure you take a full and active part
- describe a good range of leisure and tourism employment opportunities available for young people in a place or in a leisure and tourism organisation

Practice controlled assessment tasks

You might be asked to plan, carry out and report on a similar task to **one** of three below:

1 Investigate the provision of leisure and tourism facilities in your local town.

2 Investigate leisure and tourism facilities that are provided by one major leisure and tourism organisation that is:
  - either a transport provider such as a train operator
  - or a health and fitness provider

3 Investigate the range of leisure and tourism facilities in one UK seaside resort.

Requirements

Your investigation should aim to answer the following questions:
- What use do people make of leisure and tourism facilities?
- What range of leisure and tourism facilities is currently provided?
- Why is this particular range provided?
- What recent changes have taken place and are now taking place?
- Why have these changes been made?
- What range of promotional materials and techniques does **one** leisure and tourism organisation use and why?
- What range of leisure and tourism employment opportunities is available for young people?

To plan and carry out the investigation you choose you will need to:
- analyse issue(s)/problem(s)
- decide on what information to collect and how to collect it
- demonstrate your knowledge and understanding using written communication
- analyse and evaluate evidence
- make reasoned judgements
- present conclusions

Your report on your chosen investigation must:
- describe and explain how you planned and carried out your investigation
- describe the ways in which people use leisure and tourism facilities
- describe and explain the current provision of leisure and tourism facilities
- describe and explain changes that have happened over the last 20 years or so

- describe and evaluate the range of promotional materials/techniques used by one leisure and tourism organisation
- describe the range of leisure and tourism employment opportunities available for young people

Tasks **1**, **2** and **3** on page 69 are examples of the kind of tasks that might be set. The tasks change every 2 years and are published in advance on AQA's website.

Hints

Task 1 The scale of the area to be investigated should be that of a small to medium-sized town, a suburb, town or city centre or a limited rural area such as a village and its hinterland. AQA's tasks may draw on this range of possible areas.

The range of leisure and tourism facilities varies from one place to another. Deal with the range that is actually present. Explaining the range provided is part of the task.

Task 2 is about a major leisure and tourism organisation. 'Major' means that it is big enough to provide a variety of facilities. These may be on one site (such as a health and fitness club or hotel, for example).

Task 3 is set in a UK seaside resort or, sometimes, in an overseas resort. The scale is that of a resort or city, or of a defined rural area such as a National Park or Area of Outstanding Natural Beauty (as a whole or in part).

Unit 3
The business of leisure and tourism

Unit 3 is an examined unit and has a 1-hour written examination. The exam paper consists of questions that are based partly on case study material that is provided as an insert with the question paper. This material is related to one or more leisure and tourism organisations and includes mostly images with some text. The questions can be on:

- promotion and sales (marketing) in leisure and tourism
- leisure and tourism jobs and their duties, as well as the skills and qualities needed to work in leisure and tourism
- health and safety issues, and how leisure and tourism organisations deal with them

Leisure and tourism organisations operate as businesses. They market their products and services, employ people, deliver customer service and manage health and safety issues.

Providing facilities

Leisure and tourism businesses provide facilities for people to use in their local area, while they are travelling and in the destinations they visit.

You need to revise so you can:
- explain what leisure is
- explain what tourism is and the main reasons for it
- describe how people make use of leisure and tourism facilities

Leisure and tourism organisations operate facilities that include:
- leisure centres, health and fitness clubs
- theatres, cinemas, arenas, museums and galleries
- sports venues and facilities
- home-based leisure providers: computer gaming and DVD-rental shops, libraries and internet
- visitor attractions

- restaurants, cafés and take-away restaurants
- hotels and self-catering accommodation
- travel agencies and online booking websites
- tourist information centres
- transport facilities used by airline, ferry, train and coach operators and car-hire firms

You need to revise so you can:
- describe and account for the range of leisure and tourism facilities in one place
- describe and account for the range of leisure and tourism facilities that are provided by one leisure and tourism organisation

Restaurants provide facilities for people to use in their local area

Operating as a business

Leisure and tourism organisations are businesses. Each has been set up to provide a range of leisure and tourism products and services to its customers.

Some leisure and tourism businesses are privately owned, commercial enterprises. Travel agents, tour operators and hotels, for example, are usually commercial organisations. Such businesses are owned by individuals or by companies. They aim to make a profit from their activities.

Leisure and tourism businesses can also be owned by public sector or voluntary organisations:
- a leisure centre, for example, may be owned and run by the local town council
- the National Trust and the Youth Hostels Association are examples of leisure and tourism organisations that are charities

Public sector and voluntary leisure and tourism organisations are businesses too. They are established to provide a range of leisure and tourism products/services to their customers. They may not aim to make a profit but to provide:
- best value products/services to their local communities, or
- a subsidised benefit to people or the environment — to help others

Leisure and tourism organisations benefit from operating as businesses by:
- using up-to-date business systems, such as ICT systems
- promoting and selling their products/services
- recognising different attitudes and cultures among their customers
- dealing with health and safety issues

You need to revise so you can:
- explain how leisure and tourism organisations benefit from operating as businesses
- explain the importance to leisure and tourism organisations of selling products and services
- account for and evaluate the range of promotional materials and techniques used by leisure and tourism organisations

Employment opportunities

There are many different types of job in leisure and tourism. Leisure and tourism organisations employ customer service staff at different levels of seniority. Two key levels of seniority are:

- operations level: jobs that involve delivering the organisation's products/services to customers or providing customers with information about them
- management level: jobs that involve supervising operations staff

You need to know about different employment opportunities that are available in leisure and tourism at both the operational level and at the management level. You should focus very clearly on customer-fronting roles. These are roles that involve dealing with customers.

You need to revise so you can:

- describe the range of employment opportunities that are available in the leisure and tourism industry
- describe the duties of two leisure and tourism jobs
- describe the personal qualities and skills expected for leisure and tourism jobs

Topic 19
Why people use leisure and tourism facilities

What the specification requires

You need to understand why people use different leisure and tourism facilities.

In brief

People enjoy **leisure activities**. These are the fun things people do in their spare time. Watching television, reading, playing football, swimming, going to the cinema or to the theatre and cooking for pleasure are all examples of leisure activities.

People travel to destinations for **leisure tourism** — to go on holiday or to visit friends and relatives.

To take part in **leisure** activities and tourism people need to use leisure and tourism facilities.

Revision notes

Leisure facilities are places where organisations provide for people's leisure activities. Such places may be buildings (for example, a leisure centre) or outdoor sites (for example, a playing field or a sports pitch). Other examples of types of leisure facility are:

- health and fitness clubs
- swimming pools
- cinemas and theatres
- arenas and stadia
- video-rental shops and take-away restaurants

Leisure facilities are run by leisure organisations. These may be commercial companies or non-commercial organisations such as the leisure services department of the local council or voluntary groups such as sports clubs. Differences between commercial and non-commercial organisations are explained on p. 72.

In any area there will be a range of leisure facilities of various types — often a wide range.

Speak the language

leisure activity — a spare-time relaxation that is fun to do. Examples include reading, swimming and going to the cinema

leisure tourism — visiting a destination to relax and have fun, for example going there on holiday

leisure — the set of activities people enjoy in their spare time, when they are not working, sleeping or occupied with the necessities of life

Shock/Fotolia

Swimming is a popular leisure activity

Community centres are leisure facilities too. They offer a range of usually simple facilities including a function room and kitchen for hire, allowing customers to organise their own social events, such as parties. Community centres also frequently offer a programme of leisure activities in the form of classes (aerobics, for example) or clubs (ballroom dancing, for example). The purpose of community centres, which are non-commercially run, is to provide for the social welfare of the local community. In some rural areas the village hall has the same function.

Museums are leisure facilities that are also visitor attractions. Many have catering facilities such as cafés and may host arts and entertainment events, such as exhibitions of paintings or sculpture and small-scale musical performances.

Sports events take place at specialist sports venues. Catering is usually provided by fast-food outlets, bars and sometimes a restaurant. Stadia may also be hired out to host other events, such as pop and rock concerts. Many big cities (Manchester and Newcastle upon Tyne, for example) have large indoor arenas that are used sometimes for arts and entertainment events and sometimes as sports venues.

The leisure industry provides different facilities to try to meet the needs of a variety of customer types. Leisure is about how people use their spare time and people have different ideas about how to do that. They like to enjoy themselves in different ways, at different times. One person may enjoy a visit to an art gallery but another may prefer an evening out at a disco.

In a nutshell

Local leisure facilities in and around a town in the UK are likely to include:
* leisure centres and health clubs
* swimming pools and sports grounds
* parks and gardens
* libraries
* country parks and picnic sites
* museums and galleries
* theatres and cinemas
* restaurants, night-clubs and public houses

There will be others too, for example take-away restaurants and other facilities that provide for home-based leisure.

Test yourself

1 Give six examples of different types of leisure and tourism facility.

2 Explain how leisure centres and health clubs differ.

Boost your grade
Remember that leisure facilities are provided to satisfy customers' needs. Their demand for leisure activities is met by the supply of facilities. That is why your controlled assessment for the Unit 2 task asks about why people use facilities before it asks about what they provide.

Topic 20
Types of leisure and tourism organisations and facilities

What the specification requires

You need to know about different types of leisure and tourism organisations and facilities.

In brief

The range of leisure and tourism **facilities** provided in any one place varies. However, it will include some or all of the following:
- leisure centres, health and fitness clubs
- theatres, cinemas, arenas, museums and galleries
- sports venues and facilities
- home-based leisure providers — computer gaming and DVD-rental shops and libraries
- visitor attractions
- restaurants, cafés and take-away restaurants
- hotels and self-catering accommodation
- travel agencies and online booking websites
- tourist information centres
- transport facilities such as airports, ports, railway and coach stations, taxi and car-hire firms

Revision notes

Leisure and tourism facilities provide for the needs of:
- local people
- visitors

In UK towns, leisure and tourism **organisations** provide leisure and tourism facilities for both of these groups of people.

All UK towns/cities can be thought of as **tourist towns/cities** because they all have facilities that visitors use. However, those that are generally regarded as tourist towns/cities rely on tourism for their economic prosperity.

There are many different types of leisure and tourism organisation supplying leisure and tourism products and services:

Restaurateurs provide catering facilities

- sport and physical recreation providers, including local council leisure departments and health and fitness clubs
- home-based leisure providers, such as the individuals and companies who own and run computer gaming and DVD-rental shops
- entertainment providers, such as theatre and cinema operators
- visitor attraction providers
- catering and accommodation providers, such as **restaurateurs** and **hoteliers**
- travel agents and online travel bookers
- tourist information providers, including regional tourist boards
- transport providers, such as airlines, ferry companies, train and coach operators and car-hire firms

The size of leisure and tourism organisations varies from small businesses run by individuals, families or partners, to large international companies. Hotels, for example, may be run as small family enterprises or as part of a chain that can stretch around the world. Hotel companies such as Marriott and Radisson SAS are organisations that run facilities all over the world.

Speak the language

facility — a building or outside space that people use for leisure and tourism activities

organisation — a business that operates leisure and tourism facilities

tourist town/city — a town or city that is visited by many tourists and where tourism plays a major part in the local economy

restaurateurs — people who own and run restaurants. Restaurants may be run by individuals or by catering companies

hoteliers — people who own and run hotels. Hotels may be run by individuals or by companies

In a nutshell

Leisure and tourism organisations own and run leisure and tourism facilities.

There is a wide variety of leisure and tourism organisations. Every town has a range of leisure and tourism facilities.

While some towns are regarded as tourism towns/cities and others are not, all towns have facilities that meet the needs of visitors.

Test yourself

1 Give two groups of people for whom leisure and tourism facilities are provided.

2 Explain why travel and tourism facilities are provided in towns that are not normally regarded as tourist towns.

3 What does each of the following mean:
 (a) leisure and tourism organisation?
 (b) leisure and tourism facility?
 (c) leisure and tourism product/service?

Boost your grade

Be aware of similarities and differences between the ranges of leisure and tourism facilities provided by:
- a town/city that is local to you
- a tourist town/city

Be clear that a leisure and tourism organisation is the set of people (whether a family, council department or private company) that run leisure and tourism facilities.

What the specification requires

You need to understand that the UK leisure and tourism industry is changing rapidly and how it is changing.

In brief

The UK leisure and tourism industry is changing rapidly. These changes are in:

- the provision of leisure locally
- travel opportunities (such as the growth of budget airlines) and holiday booking patterns (such as the expansion of self-packaging)
- response to environmental concerns (such as the growth of ecotourism)

Revision notes

Local leisure provision

Local leisure provision in the UK has changed greatly in the last 20 years or so. There are, for example, more health and fitness clubs, more drive-through fast food outlets, more coffee-bar chains, and more restaurants that used to be traditional pubs (**gastropubs**) than there were.

Many adults have witnessed changes in leisure provision in their local area. These people are a valuable source of information about the changes that have taken place.

Types of facility that may have been affected by changes in local leisure provision over the last 20 years are:

- leisure centres
- health and fitness clubs

The last 20 years have seen a growth in leisure centres

- theatres and cinemas
- museums and art galleries
- sports facilities
- home-based leisure facilities, such as computer gaming and DVD-rental shops, libraries and internet home-based leisure providers
- restaurants, cafés and take-away restaurants

Changes in local leisure provision over the last 20 years have been broadly similar in different parts of the UK. The growth in the number of health and fitness clubs and town-centre restaurants offering different **cuisines**, and the smaller number of shops selling recorded music are changes that are repeated across the UK. They reflect current national trends in people's leisure activities:

- increased participation in health and fitness activities, such as going to the gym
- more people eating out more often
- greater use of computers and other electronic devices for leisure at home

Such trends are based on a greater awareness among the public of the health and fitness benefits of physical recreation, on increased levels of disposable income and on changes in social behaviour and technology. It is more common now than it was 20 years ago for younger people to socialise in bars, clubs and restaurants in towns and city centres — as result there are more such facilities aimed at the 18–30 age group.

There is increased **social segregation**, in terms of age, between people socialising in town-centre leisure facilities in the evening and those using similar types of facilities in the suburbs and surrounding villages. For example, pubs in town centres attract younger customers in the evening while those that are out-of-town appeal more often to older people.

Dynamic packaging on the internet

Travel opportunites

A traditional package holiday is put together by a tour operator and sold as a ready-made product either through a travel agent or directly to the customer.

Since the 1990s, the range of travel opportunities available to people has broadened. An important change has been the development of **budget airlines**, such as easyJet and Ryanair.

A key change in holiday booking patterns recently has been the expansion of **dynamic packaging**. This is also known as **self-packaging**. This change has paralleled the growth of budget airlines and the spread of the internet.

Dynamic packaging allows a customer to put together their own travel or holiday package from a menu of elements, such as air flights, transfers, car-hire, accommodation and excursions.

The internet has made dynamic packaging possible. The customer can use websites such as Expedia.co.uk to assemble a self-customised travel package for which the travel provider then charges a single price.

Self-packaging involves customers assembling the elements of their trips from a number of component parts, such as:

- travel (an air flight or a rail journey for example)
- transfer (transport from a gateway point of arrival such as an airport to accommodation)
- possible car hire
- accommodation
- excursions

The resulting self-package may include as few as two of the above or as many as all of them. It is a package because the customer pays the provider one price for the whole product.

While **tailor-made holidays** and **independent travel** already existed 20 years ago, it was not until after the advent of the internet in the 1990s that self-packaging became very important.

Changing travel opportunities (such as the growth of budget airlines) and holiday booking patterns (such as the expansion of self-packaging) have affected the UK **travel and tourism industry**. Tour operators and travel agents, for example, have changed the ways in which they do business. Similarly, hotel and self-catering accommodation providers, and transport providers such as airlines, ferry companies, train and coach operators and car-hire firms have also altered their practices.

Environmental concerns

People are more environmentally aware than they used be. There has been growing public and government concern about the negative impact of leisure and tourism on the environment, as well as on local communities in destinations. Leisure and tourism has changed in response to such growing environmental concerns through:

- more **sustainability**
- the growth of **ecotourism**

Sustainability in leisure and tourism results from the ways in which tourism and leisure organisations behave. Leisure and tourism is sustainable when organisations behave in ways that do not:

- damage the environment for the future
- harm the future of the communities who live in leisure and tourism destinations

Tourists are more aware of their impact on the environment

Sustainable leisure and tourism minimises negative economic, social and environmental impacts so that the future of the environment and of destinations and their people is protected. This is important for the economic future of destinations. Visitors will not want to travel in the future to places that have been spoilt by negative impacts of leisure and tourism in the past.

Today's leisure and tourism organisations need to behave sustainably to avoid damaging the future of destinations, their people and the environment. Examples of the ways in which today's leisure and tourism organisations are behaving sustainably are:

- airlines, train operators and coach and bus operators are using vehicles with low carbon emission engines and are arranging **carbon offset schemes**
- leisure and tourism facilities, from health and fitness clubs to hotels, are using renewable energy sources, conserving energy and water and recycling as much waste as possible
- catering and accommodation providers are using locally sourced food to avoid unnecessary transportation and damage to the environment
- employing local staff and using local suppliers in destinations to protect the economic well-being and way of life of local communities
- tour operators are providing more ecotourism holidays

Speak the language

gastropub — a public house that specialises in preparing and serving restaurant-style meals. Effectively a restaurant in a building that was a previously a pub

cuisine — a style of food and cooking that is associated with a particular part of the world, such as a country. Chinese, Italian, Moroccan and Japanese cuisines are examples

social segregation — the separation of different groups of people from each other. Gender and age are two factors that can cause people to enjoy leisure separately from people from another group

budget airline — a scheduled airline that charges relatively cheap prices

dynamic packaging — customers create their own travel package (for example, flight and accommodation) by combining trip elements they choose, usually on a website such as easyJet.com or Expedia.co.uk

self-packaging — customers assemble their own package deal from a menu of optional components

tailor-made holiday — a holiday package specially assembled to meet a customer's individual needs

independent travel — a tourist makes their own travel and accommodation arrangements

travel and tourism industry — the set of leisure and tourism organisations that provide for the needs of tourists

sustainability — the ability to sustain or conserve the environment and people's ways of life into the future

ecotourism — visiting a destination because of the appeal of its natural environment while minimising negative environmental impacts

carbon offsetting — paying someone to reduce carbon emissions for you elsewhere in the world

In a nutshell

Changes in local leisure provision have taken place in the last 20 years or so. Local people are witnesses to the changes that have happened.

Transport opportunities have broadened in recent years. The growth of budget airlines has been a key change since the 1990s.

The growth of self-packaging has been a major change in recent holiday booking patterns. This change has happened alongside the expansion of the internet and the growth of budget airlines.

Changing travel opportunities (such as the growth of budget airlines) and holiday booking patterns (such as the expansion of self-packaging) are affecting the UK's travel and tourism industry. The growth of the internet is at the root of many of these changes.

Test yourself

1 Suggest why:

  (a) there are now fewer town-centre shops selling recorded music

  (b) people eat out more often than they did 20 years ago

2 Give three current national trends in people's leisure activities.

3 (a) What is meant by 'carbon offsetting'?

  (b) Why do some transport companies operate such schemes?

4 Give two ways in which the development of the internet has affected the UK travel and tourism industry.

5 Why are there now:

  (a) fewer high street travel agent shops?

  (b) more hotel websites?

6 Give two ways in which leisure and tourism organisations are behaving sustainably.

Boost your grade

Don't take 20 years too literally. It is change over that kind of period that you need to be able to describe and explain. Be aware that some changes may already have begun 20 years ago. For example, the UK's first multiplex cinema opened more than 20 years ago — in 1985.

Compare budget and conventional air flights between the same two airports. Consider the advantages and disadvantages of each for customers.

Topic 22
Leisure and tourism organisations as businesses

What the specification requires

You need to understand that leisure and tourism organisations are run as businesses.

In brief

Leisure and tourism organisations are run as businesses. They provide a range of leisure and tourism products/services to their customers through two kinds of activities or **business operations**:

- **front-of-house** (sometimes called **front-office**) operations
- **back-office** operations

Front-of-house is the part of the business that deals directly with customers. In a hotel, for example, staff who work in reception, the restaurant, the bar or as housekeeping staff often come into direct content with the hotel's customers. These **customer-fronting** staff members are engaged in the business's front-of-house activities.

In the same hotel other business operations take place behind the scenes. Examples of these back-office functions are:

- administration — keeping records of business activities, for example
- finance — dealing with money that comes into and goes out of the business
- human resources — managing the business's employees

Back-office functions may be carried out literally in the office at the back of reception. However, in some leisure and tourism organisations they are undertaken elsewhere, perhaps in a separate head office building.

Revision notes

Leisure and tourism organisations carry out business operations using set procedures. They try to design efficient and effective ways of doing things. These

A BA member of staff helps a customer with an automatic check-in system

are the organisation's business systems. In the twenty-first century often the most efficient way of carrying out business operations is to use **ICT systems**.

Efficiency means providing products/services as quickly and as economically as possible. In providing products/services economically, businesses keep their costs to a minimum. Staff wages are one example of a business cost that can be kept low by using ICT.

Providing leisure and tourism products/services to customers as effectively as possible is important to leisure and tourism organisations. Customers receiving effective customer service are more likely to be satisfied. As a result, they are more likely to:

- spend more money, because they are relaxed and enjoying themselves
- return
- recommend the organisation to other people

Speak the language

business operations — an organisation's activities that help it provide products/services to its customers

front-of-house — business operations that take place in the view of customers

front-office — another term for front-of-house. It is usually applied to travel agents

back-office — business operations that take place out of the view of customers

customer-fronting — business activities that involve dealing directly with customers

ICT systems — ways of carrying out business operations using information and communications technology

In a nutshell

Business systems are the systems an organisation uses to help it provide its customers with products/services.

ICT systems are often more efficient and effective at helping businesses serve their customers well and as a result helping the business itself to succeed.

Test yourself

1 How do front-of-house and back-office business operations differ?

2 (a) Why are satisfied customers important to leisure and tourism organisations?

(b) Why do ICT systems help leisure and tourism organisations to satisfy their customers?

Boost your grade When you investigate business systems used by a leisure and tourism organisation, such as ICT systems, find out about back-office as well as front-of-house operations.

Topic 23
Marketing in leisure and tourism

What the specification requires

You need to understand what marketing is and why it matters to leisure and tourism organisations.

In brief

Marketing is the set of tools that leisure and tourism organisations use to bring products and services to the attention of their customers. The purpose of marketing products and services is to persuade customers to buy or use them.

Revision notes

Leisure and tourism organisations operate as businesses. They provide their customers with leisure and tourism products/services. How well they do this is a measure of their success as businesses.

Commercially-run leisure and tourism organisations seek to make profits. To do so, they need to market leisure and tourism products and services to their customers. Marketing is necessary to bring the products/services to the attention of customers and sales are needed to generate income.

Although the main aims of non-commercial public sector and voluntary leisure and tourism organisations are not to make financial profits, these organisations are still run as businesses. They try to earn sufficient income to cover as many of their costs as possible. To make a profit would be a welcome bonus, certainly for a voluntary organisation. Both public sector and voluntary organisations want to attract customers and so marketing matters to them too.

Market research questionnaires are used to find out if customers are satisfied

Leisure and tourism organisations want customers to be satisfied with the products and services they receive. If they are, they will come back for more and will tell other people how good the organisation is. This results in more customers for the organisation, and more income, if it charges for its products and services.

Customers are satisfied if they are happy with:

- the quality of products and services they receive
- the price they pay for them

Marketing makes sure that customers receive the products they want, at prices they think are fair. It also involves making sure that:

- products are promoted so that customers know about them
- products are available in places that customers can easily reach

There are four main marketing tools that leisure and tourism organisations use. These are:

- identifying a **target market** — an organisation chooses a customer type at which to aim its marketing
- **market research** — an organisation finds out who might want to buy its products/services and why
- the **marketing mix** — the combination of product, price, place and promotion that is used to entice a customer to buy
- **SWOT analysis** — how an organisation works out its strengths, weaknesses, opportunities and threats as a business to help plan its marketing

Speak the language

marketing — bringing products/services to the attention of customers so that they want to buy

target market — the customer type at which a leisure and tourism organisation aims its marketing

market research — investigating who might want to buy a leisure and tourism organisation's products/services and why

marketing mix — the combination of product, price, place and promotion that a leisure and tourism organisation uses to entice a customer to buy its products/services

SWOT analysis — how an organisation works out its strengths, weaknesses, opportunities and threats as a business to help to plan its marketing

In a nutshell

Marketing is important to leisure and tourism organisations because it enables them to provide their customers with products and services.

Boost *your grade*

Marketing is an essential step to leisure and tourism business success. The point of businesses is to provide products/services to customers and marketing is the means by which this is done.

Test yourself

1 **(a)** What is meant by 'marketing'?

(b) Why do
- commercial
- non-commercial

leisure and tourism organisations market their products and services?

2 Why is marketing important to leisure and tourism organisations?

Topic 24
Promotional materials and techniques

What the specification requires

You need to know about the promotional materials and techniques used by leisure and tourism organisations.

In brief

Promotional materials are used by leisure and tourism organisations to make people aware of their products and services to encourage sales.

Promotional techniques are the methods that leisure and tourism organisations use to distribute promotional materials. They are the means by which organisations try to make sure that customers receive promotional materials.

Revision notes

Promotional materials used by leisure and tourism organisations are:
- leaflets, brochures and flyers
- posters and other advertisements, such as **bus wraps**, printed advertisements in newspapers and magazines, and internet pop-ups
- websites
- TV and radio commercials
- **merchandise** and souvenirs

Leaflets, brochures and flyers are all forms of printed promotional material, as are posters. They are all different.
- Leaflets differ from flyers because a flyer is printed on one sheet of unfolded paper whereas a leaflet has been folded. Many leisure and tourism organisations use leaflets that have been folded twice. This makes a two-sided, three-panelled leaflet that can hold a lot of information.
- Brochures are booklets of several sheets of printed paper.
- Posters are single-sided and larger than flyers. They are usually displayed on noticeboards or stuck to billboards.
- Websites are virtual promotional materials. Many leisure and tourism organisations have their own websites. TV and radio commercials are other forms of non-printed promotional materials.

The budget airline bmi used a fleet of taxis to advertise its low fares

Some leisure and tourism organisations also use merchandise to promote their products and services. Merchandise is objects that are sold by a leisure and tourism organisation to help promote its products/services. Examples are hats, t-shirts, mugs and glasses. Souvenirs may be given to customers free of charge. Many leisure and tourism organisations, hotels for example, have souvenir pens or pencils that customers can take. The organisation's contact details are printed on souvenir items, so they become advertisements.

Speak the language

bus wrap — an advertisement, usually spray-painted, that looks as if it is wrapped around a bus or other vehicle

merchandise — objects that are sold by a leisure and tourism organisation in order to help promote its products/services

The effectiveness of promotional materials in leisure and tourism depends on their design. This includes the text, images and colours that they use.

AIDA is a method used to assess how successful a promotional material is likely to be in promoting a leisure and tourism organisation's products/services:
- **A**ttention — does it grab customers' attention?
- **I**nterest — does it capture the interest of customers?
- **D**esire — does it raise the desire of customers for the product/service?
- **A**ction — does it make clear what customers can do next to buy the product/service?

The aim of a leisure and tourism organisation's promotional activities is to make customers aware of the products/services that are provided. Promotional materials are designed to highlight the advantages of those products/services so that customers will find them attractive and sales will be made. However, it does not matter how well designed promotional materials are if customers do not receive them. Therefore, leisure and tourism organisations choose promotional techniques that they think will ensure that customers receive the materials.

Promotional techniques that leisure and tourism organisations often use are:
- advertising
- sales pitching, for example telephoning potential customers or sending them promotional e-mails
- product and promotional material placement, for example placing merchandise and souvenirs in a gift shop or displaying leaflets in another facility
- sales promotions, for example making special offers

Leisure and tourism organisations classify customers as:
- potential customers — those who might use their facilities or buy their products/services
- actual customers — those who already use their facilities or buy their products/services

Returning customers are very important to leisure and tourism businesses. Pitching special offers to actual customers is a useful technique aimed at persuading them to return. Yesterday's actual customers are also tomorrow's potential customers.

In a nutshell

Leisure and tourism attractions use a variety of promotional materials to bring their products/services to the attention of customers.

The likely effectiveness of promotional materials can be assessed using the AIDA method.

Leisure and tourism organisations use a variety of promotional techniques to help promotional materials reach customers.

Test yourself

1 List a variety of different types of promotional materials that are used by leisure and tourism organisations.

2 Give three different promotional techniques that are used by leisure and tourism organisations.

Boost your grade

Collect examples of leisure and tourism organisations' promotional materials and practice evaluating them using the AIDA method.

The promotional activities of leisure and tourism organisations include materials and techniques. While they are different in meaning, it can be difficult in practice to talk about one (advertisements, for example) without the other (advertising). So don't write about an organisation's materials first and then go on to write about techniques separately and second. You will repeat yourself.

Target markets

What the specification requires

You need to understand target markets of leisure and tourism organisations.

In brief

A leisure and tourism organisation's market is its set of potential customers. Some types of customer may be attracted to a leisure and tourism organisation's products/services, others may not.

A leisure and tourism organisation's **target market** is the group of customers most likely to be attracted to its products or services, and to whom it can sell products and services. This group is the **market segment** at which it pitches its promotional material.

Revision notes

Target marketing is used by leisure and tourism organisations to try to make sure that people who want to do so can easily obtain their products and services. Different types of customers who most want the organisation's products and services are identified. The organisation then concentrates on aiming products and services at those target customer types. In this way, time, effort and money are not wasted on promoting products and services to customers who do not want them.

Different groups of customers have different needs. For example, teenagers have different needs from retired people and sporty people different needs from the less health-conscious. These different customer groups are market segments. A circle represents the whole market and the segments, or sections, of the circle represent the different market segments. The whole market is all the customers for whom the organisation provides products and services. Leisure and tourism markets can be segmented in a number of ways, including:

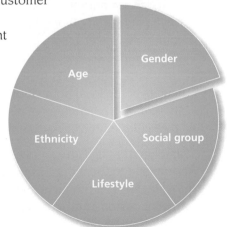

Segments in the leisure and tourism market

- *Age* — The age of a customer affects the products and services they want (or demand). Young children want different videos to their parents from a video-rental shop. To keep both groups satisfied, the shop needs to provide a range of videos for hire. National restaurant chains provide activities such as play areas and puzzles for children. This keeps their younger customers occupied, which is also a service for their parents. So, two age groups and the families market segment have been satisfied. This is part of marketing the restaurant. It means that customers are more likely to return on a future occasion and to tell other people about the service they received. The people they tell may also decide to visit the restaurant with their children and, if they enjoy their visit, tell other people, and so on.
- *Gender* — Male and female customers, even of similar ages, may have different demands. For example, some local leisure centres and health clubs provide ladies-only gym facilities, often without a male equivalent. National recreation centres offer courses and coaching geared towards a specific gender, particularly as many sports have separate male and female events and teams.
- *Social group* — Customers from a higher income bracket, with more money to spend on leisure and tourism, are likely to have demands that are different from those of less well-off people. Professional people such as senior managers, doctors and lawyers, may have requirements that are different from those of some working-class people. On a national scale, tour operators try to cater for different social groups by providing various types of holiday, to different destinations, with different grades of accommodation. Locally, leisure centres try to provide a range of activities that provide for the needs of a range of social groups.
- *Lifestyle* — The way of life people lead is connected to other factors, such as their age and the social group to which they belong. However, people from the same age and social group and of the same gender can still have different lifestyles. Home-based leisure, such as computer gaming, fits more with some people's lifestyle than do active outdoor leisure activities, such as sports. Active outdoor lifestyles are a different market segment to indoor passive lifestyles. Tour operators provide for the demands of active tourists by marketing holidays based around physical recreations such as skiing and walking.
- *Ethnicity* — Their cultural background can affect the leisure and tourism products and services that people want. In large cities some restaurants specialise in ethnic food. So, a Turkish restaurant in London may cater for customers from a Turkish background as well as for people of other ethnicities who enjoy Turkish food or who want to try something different. Travel agents in some inner city neighbourhoods specialise in flights to particular destinations such as the Caribbean or southern Asia. This is to provide for the needs of the local population, which may have a high percentage of people from a particular ethnic background.

Target marketing is the marketing tool that leisure and tourism organisations use to provide the right products and services for their different customer groups. Managers of leisure and tourism facilities ask themselves who their customers are — which of the market segments described above do they mostly belong to? Then

Speak the language

target market — the set of customers at which a leisure and tourism organisation aims its promotional activities

market segment — a division of a leisure and tourism organisation's market

grey market — the market segment of mature adults who are nearing retirement or who are recently retired

they can decide what products and services to provide. These will be products and services for which there is a demand, at a price that the customer can afford to pay and that will be sufficient to cover the facility's costs. For managers of commercial organisations, it is important to know that the prices that customers can pay will be sufficient for the organisation to make a profit. If the price for a product or service is too high for the market segment, customers will not pay and the organisation will not make money. So, the target for marketing products and services must be correctly judged.

A recent trend in leisure and tourism has been the growth of the **grey market**. This market segment consists of late-middle-aged adults who may be nearing retirement or who have recently retired. They are likely to be reasonably fit, in good health and financially well off, since their grown children have left home. The grey market is an attractive target market for leisure and tourism organisations.

The grey market is a profitable market segment

In a nutshell

Leisure and tourism organisations aim their promotional activities at identified target markets.

A leisure and tourism organisation's market is made up of different customer types.

These customer types make up the organisation's target market.

Market segmentation divides the leisure and tourism market by customer type and enables leisure and tourism organisations to identify their target markets.

The market for leisure and tourism products/services can be segmented by:
* ethnic and cultural background
* social class
* level of disposable income
* special need

Test yourself

1 What is meant by:
   (a) 'target market'?
   (b) 'grey market'?

2 Why is it important for a leisure and tourism organisation to identify its target market?

3 Identify examples of leisure and tourism organisations that target different market segments.

Boost your grade Promotional materials are aimed at certain segments of the market. Studying them can help you work out a leisure and tourism organisation's target market.

Topic 26
Working in leisure and tourism

What the specification requires

You need to know about types of jobs available in leisure and tourism.

In brief

There are many different types of job in leisure and tourism. Leisure and tourism organisations employ customer service staff at different levels of seniority. Two key levels of seniority are:

- operations level — jobs which involve delivering the organisation's products/services to customers or providing customers with information about them
- management level — jobs which involve supervising operations staff

Revision notes

Leisure and tourism organisations vary considerably, as this list of the types of organisation that you need to learn about shows:

- leisure centres and health and fitness clubs
- theatres, cinemas, arenas, museums and art galleries
- sports venues and facilities
- home-based leisure providers — computer gaming and DVD-rental shops, libraries and internet home-based leisure providers
- visitor attractions
- restaurants, cafés and take-away restaurants
- hotels and self-catering accommodation
- travel agencies and online booking websites
- tourist information centres
- airlines, ferry, train and coach operators, and car-hire firms

Speak the language

customer service roles — jobs that involve dealing directly with customers to provide them with products/services or information about them. These roles are customer-fronting roles

levels of seniority — ranks or levels of importance within an organisation. Managers are senior because they supervise operations staff who are their juniors

All these different types of leisure and tourism organisation employ people:

- in different **customer service roles**
- at different **levels of seniority**

There is therefore a very wide range of employment opportunities available in leisure and tourism.

Leisure industry jobs

Leisure centres employ leisure assistants to help customers make the most of the facilities provided. Fitness instructors may work in leisure centres or health clubs. Their duties can include demonstrating the use of gym equipment, running classes such as aerobics and designing fitness programmes for customers. Lifeguards may be based at swimming pools, including those in leisure centres, or on beaches at seaside resorts. Grounds staff may work at a sports venue such as a football or cricket stadium undertaking duties such as preparing playing surfaces for matches. Alternatively, they may be workers at a theme park where their duties, such as maintaining the tidiness of the theme park, frequently bring them into contact with customers.

Fitness instructors need to be cheerful, patient and polite with customers

Park rangers work outdoors in National Parks. They ensure that the park and its customers are properly cared for. Restaurant managers oversee the operation of a restaurant. An important aspect of their work is to manage the team of people, including waiting staff, that provide customer service to diners.

In the leisure, travel and tourism industry, jobs are available at different levels of seniority. A leisure assistant is a junior member of staff who reports to the leisure centre manager. Leisure employees on higher grades expect to be better paid than colleagues on lower grades. Opportunities for promotion may exist for junior staff who are ambitious and work well, and so career progression can be available for school- and college-leaver recruits to the leisure industry. Entering the leisure industry at a higher, managerial grade requires additional qualifications from further or higher education.

An employee's duties are those tasks that need to be completed and the responsibilities that need to be undertaken to do the job. For example, one duty of a fitness instructor in a health and fitness club might be to take new members through an induction process. An induction is an introduction that might include showing the new customer around, demonstrating the correct and safe use of equipment and helping to design a fitness programme.

Skills are what job-holders are able to do. Listening carefully to people and communicating clearly with them are examples of relevant skills for a fitness instructor.

Personal qualities are aspects of an employee's personality. The skills of a job-holder partly depend on their personal qualities. For example, the skill of listening carefully arises from the personal qualities of patience and caring. One specific personal quality required in a fitness instructor is a good memory, to remember the fitness procedures and knowledge of the products as expected of them by the health and fitness club's management. Other personal qualities needed for the job include being a team player (someone who can work well with others), confidence (to be able to teach members), as well as customer service qualities such as patience, cheerfulness, politeness and empathy with others.

Travel and tourism industry jobs

Travel consultants work in travel agencies. They advise customers about travel arrangements and holidays and make bookings for them.

A conference organiser may be based in a hotel. Larger hotels in cities are often used as venues for business meetings and conferences. The hotel's conference manager may need to coordinate several such meetings each day.

Coach drivers work in the travel and tourism industry key component of transportation. On longer tours, often the coach driver also acts as a tour guide.

Air cabin crew look after passengers' welfare on airline flights and may work on domestic, short-haul or long-haul flights.

Air cabin crew look after passengers' welfare

Tourist guides work in destinations and visitor attractions to show customers around. Such guides may be employed or work as volunteers. Some qualified Blue Badge guides in the UK are self-employed and work on a freelance basis.

Tour operators employ resort representatives. Working with out-bound tourist customers for a UK tour operator may mean that a resort representative needs to live and work abroad, at least during the main tourism season. Some resort representatives divide their year between working in a coastal Mediterranean resort in summer and in a ski resort in the Alps in winter.

In a nutshell

Leisure and tourism organisations provide a wide range of employment opportunities.

Jobs are either at operations or at management level.

Relevant leisure and tourism jobs are customer-fronting jobs.

Boost your grade When revising leisure and tourism jobs make sure that you stick rigidly to:
- jobs in leisure and tourism organisations of the types discussed on pp. 95–96
- jobs that are customer-fronting

Test yourself

1 (a) List different jobs provided by leisure and tourism organisations.

(b) Classify the jobs you have listed by level of seniority.

2 Suggest why having customer service qualities of:
- patience
- cheerfulness
- politeness
- empathy

is important for a fitness instructor.

Topic 27
Leisure industry jobs

What the specification requires

You need to know about the duties, skills and personal qualities of people in leisure industry jobs.

In brief

Some leisure industry organisations provide leisure products/services largely for the local community. They are sources of employment for local people too.

The duties of any leisure industry job are the tasks that the holder of that job must perform.

Leisure and tourism organisations know that people do well in leisure industry jobs if they have the right skills and personal qualities. When **recruitment** managers **select** new staff, they look for people who have good people skills and a positive approach to dealing with customers. Interviews are an important way in which leisure and tourism organisations assess the personal qualities of job applicants. Leisure and tourism organisations often train new staff **in-house** in the technical skills they need to do their jobs.

Revision notes

Leisure jobs are available in the following sectors of the leisure and tourism industry:
- health and fitness
- catering and hospitality

Leisure jobs and **careers** are provided by a variety of health and fitness and catering and hospitality businesses:
- leisure centres
- health and fitness clubs
- restaurants, cafés and take-away restaurants

Leisure organisations provide customer-fronting jobs at both operations and management levels. For example, in a restaurant:
- restaurant manager
- head waiter/waitress and waiting staff
- bar manager and bar staff

Erwinova/Fotolia

A restaurant manager has a customer-fronting role

Employment opportunities in catering and hospitality are found in many types of leisure and tourism facility, not just in restaurants, cafés and take-away restaurants. For example, health and fitness clubs often provide jobs in catering and hospitality.

The duties of a particular job are usually given in a **job description**. Leisure and tourism organisations give job descriptions to potential applicants for a job. Job descriptions help:

- potential applicants to decide if the job would suit them and therefore if they should apply
- employers to make clear to employees exactly what is required of them, so that the tasks required by the organisation are the tasks that are actually carried out

Speak the language

recruitment — the process of looking for new staff

select — selection is the process of choosing which people to employ

in-house — job training provided by a leisure and tourism organisation for its own staff

career — a progression of job roles in a person's working lifetime, for example from operations- to management-level roles

job description — a formal statement of what a job entails

In a nutshell

Leisure jobs are available in the health and fitness and catering and hospitality sectors of the leisure and tourism industry.

Duties are the tasks that a leisure and tourism job-holder has to do.

Both operations and management staff have duties they are required to perform.

Skills are abilities that can be learned. Leisure and tourism organisations offer training in the necessary skills to their staff.

Personal qualities are part of a person's make-up. They cannot be taught, so leisure and tourism organisations look for staff that already have the personal qualities they want when they recruit.

Personal qualities that are appropriate for working in leisure and tourism include:
* confidence
* friendliness
* cheerfulness
* calmness
* patience
* a good sense of humour

Leisure and tourism organisations are keen to recruit staff with a positive attitude to customer service. So, personal qualities are very important.

Boost your grade You need only to be able to describe the range of leisure employment opportunities in these sectors of the leisure industry:
■ health and fitness
■ catering and hospitality
■ visitor attractions

Concentrate your revision on leisure jobs in those sectors.

You need to be able to describe leisure and tourism opportunities for young people. That means people in their teens or 20s who have recently left school, college or university.

Leisure and tourism organisations look for young people who have a positive attitude to serving customers.

Test yourself

1 Explain how catering and hospitality jobs may be available in these types of leisure facility:
   ■ visitor attractions
   ■ sports and entertainment venues
   ■ transport facilities

2 Why are interviews an important way for leisure and tourism organisations to assess people's personal qualities?

Topic 28
Travel and tourism jobs

What the specification requires

You need to know about the duties, skills and personal qualities of people in travel and tourism industry jobs.

In brief

Employment opportunities in travel and tourism may be available locally or they may involve travelling or moving to another area.

Travel and tourism businesses that may offer employment opportunities are:
- visitor attractions
- retail travel agents
- transport providers
- tour operators
- accommodation providers

Revision notes

Skills and abilities

People can work in travel and tourism jobs because they have the necessary **skills** or abilities. There are two main types of skill required:
- people skills
- technical skills

People skills are those abilities needed to work with and communicate successfully with other people. These are:
- speaking clearly, politely and persuasively face-to-face and over the telephone
- listening carefully
- communicating accurately in writing

Technical skills are those skills specific to a particular job or to working in a particular leisure and tourism organisation.

Working in the travel and tourism industry requires both people and technical skills

Technical skills may include:

- using equipment safety and efficiently
- using specific pieces of computer software
- the ability to complete numerical tasks, such as calculating amounts of money
- performing set tasks and procedures as laid down by an organisation

Travel and tourism customer-fronting jobs, such as travel consultant, resort representative and hotel manager, require **personal qualities** as well as skills if they are to be done well. Organisations are keen to recruit people who have appropriate personal qualities, such as confidence, friendliness, cheerfulness, calmness, patience and a good sense of humour.

When recruiting new staff, some travel and tourism organisations see personal qualities as more important than technical skills. Such organisations prefer to select people because they have a positive attitude towards serving customers. They can train newly employed staff in the skills needed to do a job in the way the organisation wants later. This is often done through **on-the-job training**.

Travel consultants

Travel consultants advise customers about leisure and business tourism travel. Their role is to sell their employers' products/services to customers. Travel consultants work in a variety of environments:

- travel agents' shops
- travel supermarkets
- call centres
- at home

Recent changes in travel and tourism have included a reduction in the number of travel agent shops in town centres. More people are taking advantage of the internet to make their own travel arrangements. Travel agents have responded by setting up their own online booking services and call centres, and by opening out-of-town travel supermarket outlets on retail parks. These changes have affected the jobs available in **retail travel**.

Resort representatives

Resort representatives are travel and tourism employees. They work in tourism destinations and are employed by tour operators. Their role is to look after their customers':

- health, safety and security
- holiday enjoyment

In many resorts representatives work as members of a team. They need to ensure that package holiday customers are met at their point of arrival (for example, the destination's airport) and safely transferred to their accommodation. Hotel- or campsite-based representatives (or reps) organise

Resort representatives provide customers with information about their destination

welcome meetings to give customers information about the destination. Reps also use welcome meetings to promote and sell **excursions** and activities that they have organised. Promoting such **optional extra** trips is an important part of the resort representative's role. The commission earned significantly adds to the rep's income.

Resort representatives have to be on-hand or contactable throughout customers' holidays to:

- help them deal with any emergencies
- provide information
- sell and take part in optional excursions and activities

Resort reps need to ensure that customers are safely transferred to their departure airport at the end of their holiday and that they are informed of any delays.

Many resort representatives are employed on a seasonal basis. Reps for the summer season are usually recruited in the preceding autumn/winter. Successful or experienced reps are sometimes offered year-round contracts because the tour operator wants to retain its best staff.

UK-based tour operators provide employment opportunities for resort representatives overseas. Resort representatives are the face of the company in the destination. They have to be able to deal with a wide variety of customer service situations.

Hotel manager

Hotel manager is a higher-grade travel and tourism job. The job-holder is responsible for:

- the day-to-day running of a hotel and the supervision of its staff
- the hotel's services, including front-of-house operations such as reception, food and drink operations and housekeeping
- maximising the hotel's profits
- setting an example to staff by personally delivering excellent customer service

The manager of a large hotel is likely to spend much of the day in meetings with heads of departments to oversee the running of the business. However, such managers may also spend time observing staff and talking with customers to check on the delivery of customer service.

Departments in a hotel typically include:

- reception
- restaurant and catering
- conferences and meetings
- housekeeping
- maintenance

Speak the language

skill — an ability someone has gained

personal quality — an aspect of a person's personality

on-the-job training — learning a task while doing it

retail travel — organisations that sell holidays and business travel products/services directly to customers. High street travel agents are traditional retail travel providers. There are now retail travel call centres, out-of-town travel supermarkets and internet sites that also sell travel products/services

welcome meeting — a gathering of customers organised by a resort representative to provide information and promote trips and activities

excursion — a trip to a leisure and tourism destination elsewhere

optional extra — a product/service that is not included in the basic or package price which customers may choose to buy

In a smaller hotel, the manager is much more likely to be involved in the daily hands-on running of the hotel. This may include carrying out reception duties or serving meals if the need arises, for example at busy times.

In a nutshell

Travel and tourism employment opportunities are provided by a variety of different types of leisure and tourism organisation.

Resort representative is one overseas employment opportunity in travel and tourism. Hotels, for example, offer others.

Duties are the tasks that a travel and tourism job-holder has to do. Both operations and management staff, for example resort representatives and hotel managers, have duties that they are required to perform.

Test yourself

1 Choose one of the following sectors of the travel and tourism industry:
   - visitor attractions
   - retail travel
   - transport
   - tour operators
   - accommodation

List a range of employment opportunities that are available in your chosen sector.

Boost your grade Many travel and tourism employment opportunities are in the UK. UK visitor attractions and transport and accommodation providers are important sources of travel and tourism employment.

Travel and tourism organisations' own websites often have sections that give information about employment opportunities, including current vacancies and job descriptions.

2 Outline the kind of person that a resort representative job would suit well.

3 Why are welcome meetings important to resort representatives?

4 What are the differences between:
   (a) skills and qualities?
   (b) people skills and technical skills?

Topic 29
Health and safety in leisure and tourism

What the specification requires

You need to understand that leisure and tourism organisations face health and safety issues.

In brief

Leisure and tourism organisations are responsible for the health and safety of:

- customers
- staff
- the public

Revision notes

Leisure and tourism organisations must employ qualified staff who are capable of ensuring the health and safety of their customers. They need to make sure that facilities and equipment are safe to use, that food is safe to eat and that proper procedures are in place in the event of an emergency such as a fire.

Speak the language

risk — the chance of accident or mishap

Leisure activities involve an element of **risk**. Indeed for some physical activities (white-water canoeing, for example), risk is part of the fun. Leisure and tourism organisations try to keep risk to a minimum.

Leisure and tourism employees such as resort representatives (who are employed by tour operators) are responsible for the welfare of the company's customers for the duration of their holiday in a destination. This responsibility includes health and safety.

Risk is part of the fun of white-water canoeing

In a nutshell

Leisure and tourism organisations ensure the health and safety of their customers, staff and the wider public.

Ensuring the health and safety of customers helps leisure and tourism organisations to succeed as businesses.

Test yourself

1 Why do leisure and tourism organisations deal with health and safety?

2 How do leisure and tourism organisations benefit from dealing well with health and safety?

Boost your grade   While it is useful for you to realise that leisure and tourism organisations must ensure health and safety by law, you do not need to know about the various Acts of Parliament and sets of regulations that affect health and safety in leisure and tourism.

Topic 30
Managing risks

What the specification requires

You need to understand how leisure and tourism organisations manage risks.

In brief

Health and safety is important to leisure and tourism organisations.

Leisure and tourism organisations must look after the health and safety of their customers, their employees and members of the public who may be affected by their activities.

Leisure and tourism organisations take measures to ensure the health and safety of staff and customers and members of the wider public who may be affected by their activities.

Health and safety issues that leisure and tourism organisations may have to deal with include the **hazards** of:
- tripping, slipping and falling
- fire
- food poisoning
- scalding and burning from hot materials, for example in a kitchen
- injury through lifting and moving heavy objects or as a result of using dangerous equipment or from dangerous substances

Revision notes

Leisure and tourism organisations deal with health and safety because:
- it helps them as businesses
- it is morally a good thing to do
- the laws says that they must

Risk from fire is a health and safety risk that is managed by many leisure and tourism organisations.

Fire alarms and fire extinguishers are required by law

Robert Elias/Fotolia

Practical measures that a hotel may take to deal with the health and safety issue of fire include:

- training staff in evacuation procedures
- posting information notices to tell staff and customers what to do in the event of a fire
- clearly signing internal fire doors, emergency fire exits and fire escapes
- providing fire extinguishers and automatic sprays
- installing smoke alarms and fire alarms
- clearly signed evacuation meeting points
- working with and acting on the advice of the **emergency services**

Speak the language

hazard — an element of the risk posed to customers, staff or the public by a leisure and tourism facility or activity

emergency services — public services that help people in the event of an emergency. The three main emergency services are the fire, police and ambulance services

In a nutshell

Leisure and tourism organisations deal with health and safety because it matters to them as businesses. They deal with health and safety by adopting practical measures to manage risk.

Leisure and tourism organisations take measures to deal with health and safety.

Different leisure and tourism organisations may deal with similar hazards in more or less different ways.

Test yourself

1 List three hazards to leisure and tourism customers.

2 Staff are employed in a café. Identify a range of hazards that they may face.

3 How can an historic attraction such as a ruined castle pose a hazard to the public?

4 For a leisure and tourism facility you have studied or visited, list a range of hazards to:
  (a) customers
  (b) staff
  (c) the public

Boost your grade You do not need to know about the various laws and regulations that affect health and safety.

You do need to understand that leisure and tourism organisations use practical measures to deal with health and safety by managing risk.

5 Fire is one hazard to health and safety that a planned fireworks display poses.
  (a) Give two hazards to health and safety other than fire that are posed by a planned fireworks display.
  (b) Suggest a range of measures that could be taken to deal with the fire hazard.
  (c) Why would one of these measures be likely to ensure health and safety?

6 List the measures taken to deal with fire at a hotel.

7 Give two hazards that are posed to customers by paths at a visitor attraction.

Practice exam

1 How do you describe those business activities that involve staff dealing directly with customers? *(1 mark)*

2 (a) How is a flyer different from a leaflet? *(2 marks)*
(b) Name three other types of promotional material. *(3 marks)*

3 Why is it not possible to eliminate risk from leisure and tourism? *(2 marks)*

4 What is a bus wrap? *(2 marks)*

5 What does the I stand for in AIDA? *(1 mark)*

6 Outline what is meant by the 'grey market'. *(2 marks)*

7 Mailshots are unsolicited. What does 'unsolicited' mean? *(1 mark)*

8 Give two hazards that are posed to customers by footpaths at a visitor attraction. *(2 marks)*

9 Choose one leisure and tourism organisation. Evaluate either how your organisation promotes its products/services or how it deals with one health and safety issue. *(9 marks)*

10 Choose a leisure and tourism organisation.
(a) Describe the duties of two customer-fronting jobs in your organisation. *(4 marks)*
(b) Compare the personal qualities and skills needed to do these jobs. *(6 marks)*

11 What is meant by a 'customer-fronting' job? *(2 marks)*

12 Give two levels of seniority at which leisure and tourism staff work. *(2 marks)*

13 (a) What is the difference between a *skill* and a *personal quality*? *(2 marks)*
(b) Give one example of each. *(2 marks)*

14 What is:
(a) a duty? *(2 marks)*
(b) in-house training? *(2 marks)*
(c) on-the-job training? *(2 marks)*

15 Why is seasonal employment quite common in leisure and tourism? *(2 marks)*

16 What are:
(a) unsocial hours? *(2 marks)*
(b) casual work? *(2 marks)*

17 Whose health and safety are leisure and tourism organisations concerned about? *(3 marks)*

18 Explain why health and safety is important to leisure and tourism organisations. *(4 marks)*

19 Study Figure 1, which shows an announcement made at railway station.

Figure 1

(a) Outline the risk to health and safety that this announcement is about. *(2 marks)*

(b) (i) Identify three surfaces that 'may be slippery'. *(3 marks)*

(ii) Explain why the station manager made sure the announcement was made. *(5 marks)*

20 Figure 2 is a diagram showing some potential causes of risk in a fifth-floor hotel bedroom.

(a) (i) Outline two ways that the hair dryer could be a risk to health and safety. *(2 marks)*

(ii) Complete the table below.

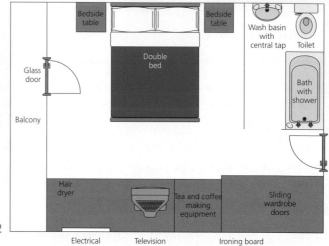

Figure 2

Potential cause	Examples of risk
Glass door to balcony	1 2
En-suite bathroom	1 2
Tea and coffee making equipment	1 2
Iron	1 2

(4 marks)

(b) Explain one other source of risk shown in Figure 2. *(3 marks)*

(c) Suggest health and safety reasons why each of the following are not provided in the hotel room shown:

(i) a rug beside the bed *(1 mark)*

(ii) a minibar. *(1 mark)*

21 Study Figure 3, a local newspaper headline.

Campsite playground is disaster zone says angry parent

Figure 3

(a) Outline two possible causes of risk in a children's playground. *(2 marks)*

(b) (i) Explain why the headline matters to the leisure and tourism organisation that operates the campsite. *(3 marks)*

(ii) Discuss the importance of the truth of the headline. *(8 marks)*

22 Choose one leisure and tourism organisation.

(a) Describe two causes of risk to the health and safety of its customers. *(4 marks)*

(b) Suggest one way in which the organisation may cause risk to the health and safety of the public. *(2 marks)*

23 Compare the level of health and safety risk faced by the organisation you chose in question 22 with that faced by another leisure and tourism organisation. *(6 marks)*

24 Evaluate the extent to which risks to health and safety are inevitable for leisure and tourism organisations. *(9 marks)*

25 Outline the range of measures taken at one leisure and tourism facility to deal with a health and safety issue other than fire. *(3 marks)*

26 Figure 4 shows information given to customers by the management of a business tourism conference facility.

FLU ALERT

Dear Guest

You will be aware from the media of recent developments regarding a flu alert in the UK. To ensure that our guests and staff are not put at any increased risk of the flu, and to avoid the spread of any viruses, we have established some brief advice notes.

To protect yourself and others from the flu, please follow good hygiene practices when you cough or sneeze.

Catch it, bin it, kill it!
- Always carry tissues
- Use clean tissues to cover your mouth and nose when you cough and sneeze
- Bin the tissue after one use
- Wash your hands regularly with soap and water or a sanitiser gel

If in doubt, call NHS Direct on 0845 4647 or seek advice from **www.nhs.uk**

Thank you for your cooperation

Figure 4

(a) (i) What is business tourism? *(2 marks)*

(ii) Outline what is meant by 'conference facility'. *(2 marks)*

(b) Explain how two of the pieces of advice in Figure 4 help ensure health and safety. *(2 marks)*

27 Discuss the importance of health and safety measures to leisure and tourism businesses.

(8 marks)

28 (a) Figure 5 shows some causes of risk to health and safety at a health and fitness club's swimming pool. Recommend and justify two practical measures that could be taken to ensure health and safety.

(6 marks)

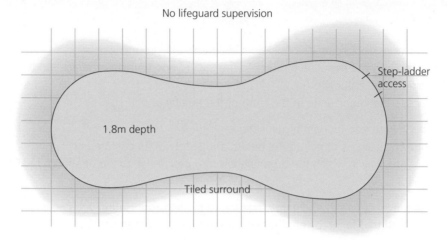

No lifeguard supervision

Step-ladder access

1.8m depth

Tiled surround

Figure 5

(b) Describe and explain two practical health and safety measures that have been taken by one leisure and tourism organisation other than at a swimming pool. *(6 marks)*

29 Figure 6 shows an information briefing given by the leader of a canoe trip for tourists along a scenic river.

Welcome to Ucan canU!

Before we set off I need you to remember these health and safety points:

- **We all stick together**
- **Keep your helmet and life jackets on**
- **Do as I ask!**

That's it. Let's go!

Figure 6

(a) Discuss whether this safety briefing is necessary. *(6 marks)*

(b) Explain what else could be included. *(4 marks)*

30 Compare how well two leisure and tourism organisations have dealt with one health and safety issue. *(6 marks)*

31 'Health and safety just gets in the way. People go to leisure and tourism facilities to have fun not be protected so much they can't enjoy themselves.'

Discuss this view. *(8 marks)*

32 Figure 7 is a photograph of a leisure club in a hotel in London.

Suggest:

(a) three leisure and tourism jobs people do in the leisure club
(3 marks)

(b) three leisure and tourism jobs people do in the rest of the hotel. *(3 marks)*

Figure 7

33 Choose one leisure and tourism job. Evaluate three personal qualities needed to do the job well. *(6 marks)*

34 Study what Gavin is saying in Figure 8.

Figure 8

(a) Recommend a leisure and tourism job for Gavin. *(1 mark)*

(b) Explain your choice. *(3 marks)*

35 Study Figure 9. Suggest how a school leaver might put her/himself in a position to apply for such a job in the future. *(4 marks)*

> **Job title:** front-of-house manager in a top conference centre.
>
> **Salary package:** attractive and competitive with healthcare, pension and company discounts.
>
> **Job description:** a top conference centre in Surrey requires an experienced front-of-house manager to successfully manage its reception, housekeeping, conference services and nights team. The successful person will have at least 2 years' experience managing a large team and be responsible for setting and maintaining high standards so that customer expectations are consistently exceeded. Hotel front-of-house management experience is desirable.

Figure 9

36 Choose one leisure and tourism job and assess how well you would suit it. *(6 marks)*

37 Study Figure 10.

Figure 10

    (a) Suggest reasons for:
- (i) choosing the photographs used on the flyer *(2 marks)*
- (ii) advertising the early and late opening and closing times. *(2 marks)*

    (b) Figure 10 is a flyer.
- (i) Give three other types of promotional material used by leisure and tourism organisations. *(3 marks)*
- (ii) What is the difference between a flyer and a leaflet? *(2 marks)*
- (iii) Suggest two promotional techniques that Willowburn Sports and Leisure Centre could use to distribute the flyer. *(2 marks)*

38 (a) Complete the table below:

Promotional materials	Promotional techniques
1	1
2	2
3	3
4	
5	

(4 marks)

    (b) Give two other sorts of promotional materials/techniques not shown in your table. *(2 marks)*

39 A small local travel agency wants to promote a new low cost, rapid currency exchange service.

    (a) Recommend two appropriate promotional techniques/materials. *(2 marks)*

    (b) Explain the choices you made in (a). *(4 marks)*

40 Study Figure 11.

    (a) Describe what the leaflet cover alone tells potential customers about the Beatles Story. *(4 marks)*

    (b) Outline three strengths of the leaflet cover as a piece of promotional material. *(3 marks)*

41 Choose a seaside or tourist town/city. Explain the content of an extended piece of promotional material you recommend to the town/city council. Choose from the following:

    (brochure)   (folding leaflet)   (display)   (website)

(6 marks)

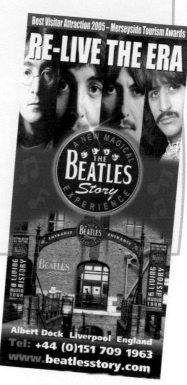

Figure 11

Unit 4
Investigating tourism destinations and impacts

Controlled assessment

This is a controlled assessment of coursework unit. It is about investigating tourism destinations and impacts. Unit 4 counts for 20% of your total marks if you are following the AQA GCSE Leisure and Tourism (Double Award) course. It is not part of the AQA Leisure and Tourism two-unit, single GCSE course.

Unit 4 is closely linked to Unit 1.

Unit 4 and Unit 1

Unit 4 is a controlled assessment unit, whereas Unit 1 is an exam unit. Unit 1 is part of both the AQA GCSE Leisure and Tourism and AQA GCSE Leisure and Tourism (Double Award) qualifications. Unit 4 is only for the Double Award.

The content of Unit 4 covers the same themes as Unit 1:
- short-haul and long-haul destinations — locations, attractions, activities, visitor types, travel options
- the impacts of tourism (on the environment and on local people)
- responsible tourism

Unit 4 is assessed differently — by controlled assessment of project work. The project you will undertake for Unit 4 will give you the chance to explore tourism destinations in more depth, since you are working towards the AQA GCSE Leisure and Tourism (Double Award) qualification.

There are examples of controlled assessment tasks for Unit 4 on page 124.

Key stages

As for Unit 2 (the other controlled assessment unit), there are three key stages in the controlled assessment process:

1 task setting — when you are set your project task
2 task taking — when you do the work to complete your set task
3 task marking — when your work is marked

What happens in each of these stages?

1 Task setting

AQA sets a choice of three tasks. You and/or your teacher will choose which one of these you will do. You may do the same one as everybody else in your class or you may not, but your task must be one of the three set by AQA. Your teacher will help you decide whether you will investigate a UK or an overseas destination(s).

For GCSE Leisure and Tourism (Double Award), AQA sets Unit 4 controlled assessment tasks every 2 years. They are published in advance on AQA's website.

Each task requires you to:

- analyse issue(s)/problem(s)
- decide what information to collect and then collect it
- demonstrate your knowledge and understanding using written communication
- analyse and evaluate evidence
- make reasoned judgements
- present conclusions

Tasks are divided into parts called strands. Each strand addresses one of the criteria used to assess your work. These are called assessment criteria. There are six assessment criteria for each controlled assessment unit. The strands cover all three Assessment Objectives (AO) of the course. Assessment Objectives describe what you should be able to do when you have finished your course. In the context of the controlled assessment units they are:

- AO1 — select and communicate knowledge and understanding.
- AO2 — apply skills, knowledge and understanding in planning and carrying out investigations and tasks.
- AO3 — analyse and evaluate information, source and evidence, make reasoned judgements and present conclusions.

2 Task taking

You will have some lessons about the unit before you begin to do the task itself. You may have already completed Unit 1, which covers the same content. You might go on a visit or a speaker may visit your centre. You should make sure that you know and understand the assessment criteria for the unit before you start. These are the parts that make up the whole project. You will be marked according to how well you have completed each assessment criterion. The assessment criteria for Unit 4 are explained below. Those for Unit 2 were explained earlier.

Your project task for Unit 4 should take you about 45 hours to complete. This includes preparation time (going on a visit, for example) but not lesson time spent on learning about the unit's content. This is a guideline figure only. It is a good idea to spend equal amounts of time on each of the six assessment criteria for Unit 4, although Strand B (worth significantly fewer marks) should take a shorter time. It is also a good idea to complete one assessment criterion at a time, writing each up as you go rather than waiting until the end and having to do them all at once.

Most students use a word processor for their work, but it is not necessary. Handwritten work is perfectly acceptable.

Your research will be done under 'limited supervision'. Limited supervision means that your teacher will keep an eye on what you are doing but you can collect information independently. You can do that in small groups, providing each group member's role is clear and you can demonstrate that you took an active part.

Once you have done your research, you will be under 'informal supervision'. Informal supervision means that you do not have to write up your work under examination conditions but it also means that your teacher will check that:

- you have not plagiarised your work (for example, copied it from someone else, from a book or copied and pasted unacknowledged sections of websites)
- you have clearly recorded the sources you have chosen and used
- your work is your own
- you have completed the task as set by AQA

Your teacher can give you guidance while you are writing up your work, but this will be limited. Your teacher can advise you how to approach your work, check it and can give you general feedback, but cannot tell you exactly how to rewrite bits to score higher marks. Any guidance your teacher does give you has to be recorded on the front sheet (Candidate Record Form) of your work and sent to AQA. Your teacher can tell you how well you are doing and suggest general ways to improve but cannot give you detailed corrections and suggestions. That would be breaking the rules.

While you are doing your research, you should keep notes to help you when writing up your work. It is good to include primary and secondary sources of information.

Primary sources are those you have used to gather information yourself, for example by using questionnaires, surveys, interviews or observation.

Secondary sources are those you have used to look up information collected by others. They include promotional materials, books, maps and websites.

You must clearly reference all the sources you have used. A bibliography is a good idea.

Your research notes will be kept by your teacher and sent to AQA if requested.

3 Task marking

Your teacher will mark your work. The assessment criteria will be used to decide what score your teacher thinks you should have (not what grade). AQA will check your teacher's marking to make sure that every student is treated the same, no matter which teacher they had. This is called moderation. AQA will decide on the grade for your work.

Assessment criteria

Strand A

Strand A is about planning and carrying out your investigation.

As for all strands, Strand A is assessed against three levels of quality. Your teacher will score your finished work within one of these three levels.

Level 1 (up to 5 marks)

To gain a Level 1 score for Strand A you should outline how you went about collecting and recording your evidence.

You should also:
Give reasons why you went about it the way you did.

Level 2 (6 to 10 marks)

At this level, you will:

- clearly identify the evidence that you have collected
- clearly describe (in sentences and paragraphs, *not* lists and bullet points) how you collected your evidence and how you recorded it

You should also:
Clearly explain (in sentences and paragraphs, *not* lists and bullet points) you used the methods you did.

Level 3 (11 to 15 marks)

At this level, you will:

- clearly identify the evidence that you have collected, and
- describe in detail (as fully as you can, in sentences and paragraphs) how you collected your evidence and how you recorded it

You should also:
Fully justify the methods you used (explain in detail why they were the correct/best methods, in sentences and paragraphs).

To get the maximum marks in Strand A:

- make sure you understand exactly what you are doing and why you are doing it
- keep a careful record of all the information you collect, including when and where you found it
- if you are working in a group, take a full and active part
- include examples of data collecting sheets (not every one – just examples) in your finished work
- do not write all of this strand up immediately – it will be easier to give reasons for/explain/justify your methods when you see the outcome of your research
- so, finish writing up Strand A at the end

Strand B

Strand B is about the location of your chosen destination. If your chosen destination is inside the UK, you will look at its location in relation to where you live. If it is an overseas destination, you will look at its location in relation to the UK and you should refer to how far away from the UK your destination is in distance and time.

Maps will be useful and will help you to write a good description.

Unlike other strands, Strand B is assessed against only two levels of quality. Your teacher will score your finished work within one of these two levels.

Level 1 (up to 4 marks)

To gain a Level 1 score for Strand B you should describe (in sentences, *not* bullet-points) where your chosen destination is located.

Level 2 (5 to 8 marks)

At this level, you should describe *clearly* (using sentences and paragraphs, *not* bullet-points) where your chosen destination is located.

To get the maximum marks in Strand B:

- make sure you understand exactly what you are doing
- at all times write in sentences and paragraphs, never in bullet point lists
- if you are working in a group, take a full and active part
- include time and distance in your description
- use maps to help you make your points

Strand C

Strand C is about the suitability of attractions and activities available in your chosen destination. Who or what they are suitable for will depend upon the task set and the option you have chosen from the task menu.

You might prefer to do the work for Strand C *after* you do Strand D. This is because Strand D is about the suitability of travel options to the destination. You might think it is logical to deal with those before considering the suitability of what is available there, as Strand C asks.

As for all strands, Strand C is assessed against three levels of quality. Your teacher will score your finished work within one of these three levels.

Level 1 (up to 5 marks)

To gain a Level 1 score for Strand C you should outline (try to use sentences, *not* bullet points) *some* attractions *and/or* activities that are available in your chosen destination.

You should also:
Make some comments about the suitability of these attractions *and/or* activities.

Level 2 (6 to 10 marks)

At this level, you will need to describe (clearly, using sentences and paragraphs, *not* bullet points) *and* comment on the suitability of a *variety* of attractions *and* activities that are available in your chosen destination.

You should also:
Draw some conclusions about what attractions *and* activities are provided in your chosen destination and why.

Level 3 (11 to 15 marks)

At this level, you will analyse and evaluate the suitability of a *variety* of attractions *and* activities that are available in your chosen destination. That means consider and explain the range of attractions and activities in classified sections (type of attraction for example), *as well as* explaining *how* suitable they are and why.

You should also:
- draw valid conclusions about what attractions *and* activities are available in your chosen destination and how suitable they are
- fully justify your conclusions

To get the maximum marks in Strand C:
- do it after Strand D
- make sure you understand exactly what you are doing
- at all times write in sentences and paragraphs, never in bullet point lists
- if you are working in a group, take a full and active part
- describe and exemplify the full range of attractions *and* activities that are available in your chosen destination. Try to include *examples* of all the types of attractions that are available there.

Strand D

Strand D is about suitability of attractions and activities that are available in your chosen destination. Who or what they are suitable for will depend upon the task set and the option you have chosen from the task menu.

You might prefer to do the work for Strand D *before* you do Strand C and immediately after Strand B. This is because Strand D is about the suitability of travel options to your destination and Strand B is about where the destination is located. You might think it is logical to deal with travel options before considering the suitability of what is available there, as Strand C asks.

However, do not try to do the two strands together. It doesn't work! Do one strand, then the other, and write up each completely independently within separate sections of your finished project.

As for most strands, Strand D is assessed against three levels of quality. Your teacher will score your finished work within one of these three levels.

Level 1 (up to 5 marks)

To gain a Level 1 score for Strand D you should describe (using sentences, *not* bullet points) *some* travel options that are available to your chosen destination.

Level 2 (6 to 10 marks)

At this level, you should explain *clearly* (using sentences and paragraphs, *not* bullet points) the suitability of a *variety* of travel options that are available to your chosen destination.

You should also:
Draw some conclusions about the suitability of these travel options.

Level 3 (11 to 15 marks)

At this level, you must evaluate *in detail* (use full sentences and paragraphs to explain how suitable they are) a *variety* of travel options that are available to your chosen destination.

You should also:
- draw conclusions about the suitability of these travel options
- fully justify your conclusions

To get the maximum marks in Strand D:

- do it after Strand B and before Strand C
- make sure you understand exactly what you are doing
- at all times write in sentences and paragraphs, never in bullet point lists
- if you are working in a group, take a full and active part
- try to include *examples* of the types of travel option that are available and are actually used by significant numbers of people to reach your destination

Strand E

Strand E is about the impacts of your recommended package or travel programme or holiday on your chosen destination's local community and on the environment, depending on which task option you have chosen.

You might prefer to complete the work for Strands B, C and D *before* you do Strand E. This is because Strands C and D are about travel options and tourism destination attractions and activities that all have an impact. You might think it is logical to know about them before considering what their impacts are, as Strand E asks. It is also sensible to do Strand B before Strand D.

However, do not try to do two or more strands together. It doesn't work! Do one strand, then the other and and write up each completely independently within separate sections of your finished project.

As for most strands, Strand E is assessed against three levels of quality. Your teacher will score your finished work within one of these three levels.

However, you should also be aware that Strand E is used to assess the quality of your written communication (how well you use written English to put across your knowledge and understanding). Of course, you should always use your best English, but it is especially important that you do so here.

Level 1 (up to 5 marks)

To gain a Level 1 score for Strand E you should describe (using sentences, *not* bullet points) *some possible* impacts of your recommended package or travel programme or holiday on your chosen destination's local community and on the environment.

You should also:
- use *some* specialist leisure and tourism terms that you have learned from your course
- write legibly, so your work can be read easily
- use your best spelling and grammar, and check both

Level 2 (6 to 10 marks)

At this level, you will need to describe *clearly* (using sentences and paragraphs, *not* bullet points) *some likely* impacts of your recommended package or travel programme or holiday on your chosen destination's local community and on the environment.

You should also:
- evaluate these *likely* impacts
- use a *good range* of specialist leisure and tourism terms that you have learned from your course
- write legibly, so your work can be read easily
- use your best spelling and grammar, and check both

Level 3 (11 to 15 marks)

At this level, you should analyse and evaluate *in detail* (using full sentences and paragraphs) a *variety* of positive and negative impacts of your recommended package or travel programme or holiday on your chosen destination's local community and on the environment.

You should also:

- draw conclusions and justify them
- use a *wide range* of specialist leisure and tourism terms that you have learned from your course
- write legibly, so your work can be read easily
- use your best spelling and grammar, and check both

To get the maximum marks in Strand E:

- do it after Strands B, D and C (Strand B first, then D, then C)!
- make sure you understand exactly what you are doing
- at all times write in sentences and paragraphs, never in bullet point lists
- if you are working in a group, take a full and active part
- include a full range of positive and negative impacts of your recommended package or travel programme or holiday on your chosen destination's local community and on the environment

Strand F

This is the sixth Strand for Unit 4. Depending on the order in which you have done the others, this may be the last Strand you have to complete. Strand F is about why your recommended package or travel programme or holiday is an example of responsible tourism.

Responsible tourism is way of behaving when travelling to and visiting destinations. Responsible tourists seek to maximise the positive impacts of their holiday, including their travel, on the environment and on local people, while minimising the negative ones.

You might prefer to complete the work for Strand E *before* you do Strand F. This is because Strand E is about the impacts of your recommended package or travel programme or holiday. You might think it is logical to know about those before explaining why your recommendation is an example of responsible tourism, as Strand F asks.

As for most strands, Strand A is assessed against three levels of quality. Your teacher will score your finished work within one of these three levels.

Level 1 (up to 4 marks)

To gain a Level 1 score for Strand F you need to describe (using sentences, *not* bullet points) what responsible tourism is *and* make links between responsible tourism and your recommended package or travel programme or holiday.

Level 2 (5 to 8 marks)

At this level, you should explain *clearly* (using sentences and paragraphs, *not* bullet points) why your recommended package or travel programme or holiday is an example of responsible tourism.

Level 3 (9 to 12 marks)

At this level, you must explain *in detail* (using full sentences and paragraphs) why your recommended package or travel programme or holiday is an example of responsible tourism.

To get the maximum marks in Strand F:

- do it after Strand E
- make sure you understand exactly what you are doing
- at all times write in sentences and paragraphs, never in bullet point lists
- if you are working in a group, take a full and active part

Practice controlled assessment tasks

You may be asked to plan, carry out and report on a task similar to **one** of the three below:

1 Design an ecotourism holiday to one overseas tourism destination that would be suitable for tourists from the UK.

2 Propose a travel itinerary for an independent traveller who wants to behave as a responsible tourist while visiting a long-haul destination. Justify the itinerary you propose.

3 Plan a responsible tourism holiday, including travel arrangements, to a UK leisure and tourism destination for a retired couple from another country. Explain why your holiday plan would be suitable for them.

Requirements

Your investigation should aim to answer the following questions:
- Where is the chosen destination?
- What attractions and activities are involved?
- What are suitable travel arrangements?
- What tourism impacts will the proposed holiday or travel itinerary be likely to have?
- Why is the proposed holiday or travel itinerary responsible tourism?

To plan and carry out the investigation you choose you will need to:
- analyse issue(s)/problem(s)
- decide on what information to collect and how to collect it
- demonstrate your knowledge and understanding using written communication
- analyse and evaluate evidence
- make reasoned judgements
- present conclusions

Your report on your chosen investigation must:
- describe and explain how you planned and carried out your investigation
- describe the location of the destination you have chosen
- explain the suitability of attractions and activities
- explain the appropriateness of travel arrangements
- assess the likely tourism impacts of the proposed holiday or travel itinerary
- explain why the proposed holiday or travel itinerary is responsible tourism

Tasks **1**, **2** and **3** above are examples of the kind of tasks that might be set. The tasks change every 2 years and are published in advance on AQA's website.

Hints

When describing the location of the destination, clearly state where in the UK it is located or, if abroad, where it is relative to the UK. Use a map or maps to illustrate its location. You might describe how far a UK destination is from where you live and how long it would take to travel there. For a destination abroad you might describe how far it is from the UK and how long it would take to travel there.

When you explain why travel arrangements are suitable, make sure that you include transport modes, routes, providers and prices.

When assessing impacts, think about impacts on the environment and on people who live in the destination. Include the impact of travelling to the destination.

Task 1 The destination could be a short-haul destination (in Europe or the Mediterranean Basin) or it could be further afield (long-haul). Obviously it must be a destination that is appropriate to ecotourism (defined as travel to a place because of its natural environment while minimising negative impacts on that environment). Attractions, activities and travel arrangements all have to be suitable for an overseas ecotourism holiday.

Task 2 The chosen destination must be a long-haul one. It could be in North or South America, the Caribbean, Africa, Asia, Australasia or Antarctica. Indian or Pacific Ocean island destinations are other possibilities. The itinerary should be appropriate for an independent traveller who is a responsible tourist.

Task 3 The chosen leisure and tourism destination must be in the UK. A holiday suitable for a retired couple from abroad is needed.

Speak the language index